An Englishman's Travels in America

John Benwell

Contents

AN ENGLISHMAN'S
TRAVELS IN AMERICA

BY

John Benwell

PREFACE.

Personal narrative and adventure has, of late years, become so interesting a subject in the mind of the British public, that the author feels he is not called upon to apologize for the production of the following pages.

It was his almost unremitting practice, during the four years he resided on the North American continent, to keep a record of what he considered of interest around him; not with a view to publishing the matter thus collected, for this was far from his thoughts at the time, but through a long contracted habit of dotting down transpiring events, for the future amusement, combined, perhaps, with instruction, of himself and friends. It therefore became necessary, to fit it for publication, to collate the accumulated memoranda, and select such portions only as might be supposed to prove interesting to the general reader. In doing this he has been careful to preserve the phraseology as much as possible, with a view to give, as far as he could, something like a literal transcript of the sentiments that gave rise to the original minutes, and avoid undue addition or interpolation.

It was the wish and intention of the writer, before leaving England, to extend his travels by visiting some of the islands in the Caribbean Sea, a course which he regrets not having been able to follow, from unforeseen circumstances, which are partially related in the following pages. He laments this the more, as it would have added considerably to the interest of the work, and enabled him to enlarge upon that fertile subject, the relative position at the time of the negro race in those islands, and the demoralized condition of their fellow-countrymen, under the iniquitous system of slavery, as authorized by statute law, in the southern states of America. As it was, he was enabled to travel through the most populous parts of the states of New York and Ohio, proceeding, *via* Cincinnati, to the Missouri country; after a brief stay at St. Louis, taking the direct southern route down the Missouri and Mississippi rivers, to New Orleans in Louisiana, passing Natchez on the way. The whole tour comprising upwards of three thousand miles.

From New Orleans he crossed an arm of the Gulf of Mexico to the Floridas, and after remaining in that territory for a considerable time, and taking part under a sense of duty in a campaign (more to scatter than annihilate), against the Seminole and Cherokee tribes of Indians, who, in conjunction with numberless fugitive slaves, from the districts a hundred miles round, were devastating the settlements, and indiscriminately butchering the inhabitants, he returned to Tallahassee, taking stage at that town to Macon in the state of Georgia, and from thence by the Greensborough Railway to Charleston in South Carolina, sailing after rather a prolonged stay, from that port to England.

Some of the incidents related in the following pages will be found to bear upon, and tend forcibly to corroborate, the miseries so patiently endured by the African race, in a vaunted land of freedom and enlightenment, whose inhabitants assert, with ridiculous tenacity, that their government and laws are based upon the principle, "That all men in the sight of God are equal," and the wrongs of whose victims have of late been so touchingly and truthfully illustrated by that eminent philanthropist, Mrs. Stowe, to the eternal shame of the upholders of the system, and the fearful incubus of guilt and culpability that will render for ever infamous, if the policy is persisted in, the nationality of America.

Well may the benevolent Doctor Percival in his day have said, when writing on the iniquitous system of slave holding and traffic, that "Life and liberty with the powers of enjoyment dependent on them are the common and inalienable gifts of bounteous heaven. To seize them by force is rapine; to exchange for them the wares of Manchester or Birminghan is improbity, for it is to barter without reciprocal gain, to give the stones of the brook for the gold of Ophir."

CHAPTER I.

"Adieu, adieu! my native shore
Fades o'er the waters blue,
The night-winds sigh, the breakers roar,
And shrieks the wild sea-mew.
Yon sun that sets upon the sea
We follow in his flight;
Farewell awhile to him and thee,
My native Land--Good night!"--BYRON.

Late in the fall of the year 18--, I embarked on board the ship *Cosmo*, bound from the port of Bristol to that of New York. The season was unpropitious, the lingering effects of the autumnal equinox rendering it more than probable that the passage would be tempestuous. The result soon proved the correctness of this surmise, for soon after the vessel departed from Kingroad, and before she got clear of the English coast, we experienced boisterous weather, which was followed by a succession of gales, that rendered our situation perilous. But a partial destruction of the rigging, the loss of some sheep on the deck of the vessel, and a slight indication of leakage, which was soon remedied by the carpenter of the ship and his assistants, were happily the only detrimental consequences arising from the weather.

Our progress on the whole was satisfactory, although, when we arrived between 48 and 52 degrees north latitude, we narrowly escaped coming in contact with an enormous iceberg, two of which were descried at daybreak by the "lookout," floundering majestically a little on the ship's larboard quarter, not far distant, the alarm being raised by an uproar on deck that filled my mind with dire apprehension, the lee bulwarks of the vessel were in five minutes thronged with half-naked passengers, who had been roused unexpectedly from their slumbers, staring in terror at the frigid masses which we momentarily feared would overwhelm the ship. The helm being put up, we were soon out of the threatened danger of a collision, which would have consigned us to a grave in the wide wide waters, without the remotest chance of escape. This consideration was, to all on board, a matter of deep thankfulness to the mighty Author of such stupendous wonders, who had so miraculously preserved our lives. Had the adventure occurred in the night, our destruction must have been inevitable, as the ship was sailing under heavy canvas, within a single point of the wake of one of the icebergs, which was drifting before a stiff breeze.

Although this encounter proved harmless, we shortly after had another to dread of a fearful nature. The number of fishing-boats off the coast of Newfoundland, makes the navigation perilous at almost any time to vessels approaching too near the banks, and after night-fall, the vessel going at the rate of ten knots an hour with a smacking breeze, we passed many of these at anchor, or rather, I suppose, riding on the waves; they displayed lights, or serious consequences might have ensued. Some of the skiffs were so near to us, that as I leaned over the ship's quarter-rail, dreading, and every moment expecting, that we should run one down, I could distinctly hear the crews hailing us to shorten sail and keep off. By adopting this course our vessel cleared the danger, and after slightly touching the banks, which caused the vessel to heel, and created a momentary panic on board amongst the passengers, she was steered more out to sea, and by the following morning nothing was to be seen but a boundless waste of waters, extending as far as the eye could reach.

After these temporary alarms, with the exception of baffling winds, which impeded the progress of the ship, and lengthened the duration of our confinement ten days or a fortnight, our voyage was prosperous, little occurring to break the monotony of confinement on ship-board that is experienced in sea-passages in general; the only excitement being a fracas between the captain and cook, owing to complaints made by the middle-cabin and steerage passengers, which nearly ended fatally to the former, who would have been stabbed to a certainty, but for a by-stander wresting the knife from the hand of the enraged subordinate, who had been supplied too liberally with spirits by the passengers; a predominating evil on board all emigrant ships, from the drawback of duty allowed on spirits shipped as stores, and which are retailed on the voyage to the passengers. The culprit was confined below during the remainder of the voyage, and when we arrived at New York presented a pitiable sight, having been rigidly debarred by the captain's orders of many of the commonest necessaries, I believe, the whole time. Here he was released and discharged from the ship, glad enough to escape further punishment, "prosecution" having been, since the occurrence, held *in terrorem* over him.

It was late in the afternoon of an intensely cold day, which caused the spray to congeal as it dashed against the bulwarks and cordage of the vessel, that we descried with great pleasure looming indistinctly in the distance, the shores of Sandy Hook, a desolate-looking island, near the coast of New Jersey, about seven miles south of Long Island Sound. This the captain informed me was formerly a peninsula, but the isthmus was broken through by the sea in 1767, the year after the declaration of American independence, an occurrence which was at the time deemed ominous of the severance of the colonies from the mother country, and which proved in reality to be the precursor of that event.

The sight of *terra firma*, though at a distance and but gloomy in aspect, put all on board in buoyant spirits; but these were but transitory, our enthusiasm being soon damped by a dense fog, resembling those the Londoners are so accustomed to see in the winter, and which in an incredibly short space of time, in this instance, obscured everything around. Our proximity to the shore rendered the circumstance hazardous to us, and it appeared necessary that the vessel's head should be again put seaward; but this the captain was evidently anxious to avoid, as it involved the risk of protracting the voyage. A general rummage for ammunition was therefore ordered, and a supply of this necessary having been obtained, the ship's carronade was after considerable delay put in order, and minute guns were fired. After discharging some thirty rounds or more, we were relieved from the state of anxiety we were in by a pilot hailing the ship, and in a minute after he was on deck issuing orders with great pertinacity.

It is impossible for any one unaccustomed to sea voyages to form a just conception of the relief afforded by the presence of that important functionary, a pilot. Perhaps a captain's greatest anxiety is, when his vessel, having braved a thousand perils on the deep, is about to enter on the termination of its voyage. On the broad expanse of ocean, or, in nautical phrase, with plenty of sea-room, if his bark is in good condition, he fears little or nothing, but when his vessel approaches its goal, visions of disaster arise before him, and he becomes anxious, thoughtful, and taciturn.

The pilot informed us that he had kept our vessel in chase for a considerable time, and had burnt a number of newspapers on the deck of his cutter to attract attention, but all his efforts proved unavailing, when just as he was about to abandon the pursuit, he descried and hailed the ship. This being the first specimen of an American whom many of the passengers had seen in his native climate, their curiosity was aroused, and they crowded round him, regarding every word and movement with the greatest attention and interest. The pilot was evidently displeased with being made "a lion" of, and gave vent to his feelings rather freely, while there was a curl of hauteur on his lip, that indicated a species of contempt for the company he was in. This disposition did not convey a very favourable idea of his countrymen, and was, to say the least of it, an ill-judged display before strangers; coming, however, as it did, from an illiterate man, belonging, as I knew from previous inquiry, to rather an exceptional class of individuals in America, I did not suffer my mind to be biassed, although I could see that many of the passengers were not disposed to view the matter in the same light. He was a brusque and uncouth man, of swaggering gait, about forty years of age, above the middle stature, and soon let the captain and crew know, by his authoritative manner and volubility of tongue, that he was chief in command on the occasion. No one seemed, however, to dispute this, for the passengers looked on him as a sort of divinity sent to their rescue; the ship's hands were implicitly obedient, and the captain very soon after his arrival retired into the cabin, glad to be relieved from a heavy responsibility.

The following morning, the haze having cleared off, we could again see the Jersey shore. The sea in every direction was now darkened with millions of black gulls, wild ducks, and other aquatic birds; we shot many of these from the ship's deck, but were, much to our mortification, obliged to see them drift away, the pilot, seconded by our austere captain, strenuously objecting to a boat being lowered; this was very discouraging, as such a change in our diet would, after a rather prolonged voyage, have been acceptable.

A favourable breeze soon carried our good ship to the quarantine ground, where we dropped anchor, in no little anxiety lest we should be detained. The medical officers from the college, or rather sanatory establishment, on shore, almost immediately came on board. All hands were mustered on deck, and ranged like soldiers on parade ground by these important functionaries, who, I may remark by the way, appeared like our pilot to be possessed of considerable notions of power and authority. After taking a rather cursory inspection they left the vessel, and we, to our great joy (a case of small pox having occurred during the passage), were allowed to proceed towards New York, which we did under easy sail, the breeze rendering a steam-tug unnecessary.

The scenery as we passed up the river was calculated to give a good impression of the country, the zest being, however, without doubt, greatly heightened by the monotonous dreariness of a tempestuous voyage. The highlands and valleys, as we sailed up, had a verdant woody appearance, and were interspersed with rural and chateau scenery; herds of cattle remarkable for length of horn, and snow-white sheep, were grazing placidly in the lowlands. The country, as far as I could judge, seemed in a high state of culture, and the farms, to use an expression of the celebrated Washington Irving's, when describing, I think, a farm-yard view in England, appeared "redolent of pigs, poultry, and sundry other good things appertaining to rural life."

On arriving at the approach to the entrance or mouth of the river Hudson, which is formed by an arm of the estuary, we turned the promontory, leaving Jersey on the left, the battery as we entered the harbour being in the foreground. The guns-bristled from this fortress with menacing aspect, and the sentinels, in light blue uniforms and Kosciusko caps, silently paced the ramparts with automatic regularity. This fortification, though formidable in appearance, and certainly in a commanding position, I was subsequently informed is little more than a mimic fort; this arises from the want of attention paid to defences of the kind in America, the little existing chance of invasion, perhaps, causing the indifference to the subject. If, however, the spirit of aggressive conquest shown by the federal government, of late years, of which the invasion of Mexico is a fair specimen, should continue to develop itself, it is not difficult to foresee that it will be necessary policy to pay greater attention to the subject, and to keep in a more effective state the seaboard defences of the country, as well as their army, which is at present miserably deficient. This has heretofore been so far neglected, as regards the marine, that not long before I arrived the commander of a French ship of war was much chagrined, on firing a salute as he passed the battery at New York, to find that his courtesy was not returned in the customary way. He complained of the omission as either a mark of disrespect to himself, or an insult to his nation, when it came out in explanation that the garrison was in such a defective state that there were not the appliances at hand to observe this national etiquette.

The city of New York is built almost close to the water's edge, with a broad levee or wharf running round a great portion of it. Its general appearance gives to a stranger an impression of its extent and importance. It has been aptly and accurately described as a dense pack of buildings, comprising every imaginable variety, and of all known orders of modernized architecture. The tide flows close up to the wharves which run outside of the city, and differs so little in height at ebb or flow, that vessels of the largest class ride, I believe, at all times as safely as in the West India docks in London, or the imperial docks of Liverpool. Here was assembled an incalculable number of vessels of all sizes and all nations, forming a beautiful and picturesque view of commercial enterprise and grandeur, perhaps outvying every other port in the world, not excepting Liverpool itself.

As our vessel could not at once be accommodated with a berth, owing to the crowded state of the harbour, she was moored in the middle of the stream, and being anxious to go on shore, I availed myself of the captain's offer to take me to the landing-place in his gig. We went on shore in an alcove, at the foot of Wall-street, and I experienced the most delightful sensation on once more setting foot on ***terra firma***, after our dreary voyage. The day, notwithstanding it was now October, was intensely hot (although a severe frost for two or three days before gave indications of approaching winter), and the streets being unmacadamized, had that arid look we read of in accounts of the plains of Arabia, the dust being quite deep, and exceeding in quantity anything of the kind I had ever seen in European cities: clouds of it impregnated the air, and rendered respiration and sight difficult.

Hundreds of rudely-constructed drays were passing to and fro, heavily laden with merchandize, many of them drawn by mules, and the remainder by very light horses of Arabian build; the heavy English dray horse was nowhere to be seen, the breed as I afterwards learned not being cultivated, from a dislike to its ponderousness.

The lower part of Wall-street presented a busy mart-like appearance, every description of goods being piled heterogeneously before the warehouse-doors of their respective owners in the open thoroughfare, which is at this part very wide. Auctioneers were here busily engaged in the disposal of their merchandise, which comprised every variety of produce and manufacture, home and foreign, from a yard of linsey-woolsey, "hum spun" as they termed it, to a bale of Manchester long cloth, or their own Sea-Island cotton. The auctioneer in America is a curious specimen of the biped creation. He is usually a swaggering, consequential sort of fellow, and drives away at his calling with wondrous impudence and pertinacity, dispensing, all the while he is selling, the most fulsome flattery or the grossest abuse on those who stand around. One of these loquacious animals was holding forth to a crowd, just below the ***Courier and Inquirer*** newspaper office, where the street widens, as a preliminary introduction to the sale of a quantity of linen goods that had been damaged at a recent fire in the neighbourhood. I could not help admiring the man's tact. Fixing his eyes on an individual in a white dress, with an enormous Leghorn hat on his head, who was apparently eagerly listening, while smoking a cigar, to the harangue, he suddenly exclaimed, "There now is Senator Huff, from the State of Missouri, he heerd of this vendue a thousand mile up river, and wall knows I'm about to offer somethin woth having; look at him, he could buy up the fust five hunderd folks hed cum across anywhar in this city, and what's more, he's a true patriot, made o' the right kinder stuff, I guess."

He followed up the eulogium at great length, and after liberally dispensing "soft soap" on the listeners, declared the auction had commenced. I stood by for some minutes, gazing around and watching the operations, and was not long in discovering that Senator Huff kept running up the articles by pretended bids, and was evidently in league with him, in fact a confederate. This auctioneer was the very emblem of buffoonery and blackguardism; the rapidity with which he repeated the sums, supposed by the bystanders to be bid, the curt yet extravagant praise bestowed on his wares, and his insulting and unsparing remarks if a comment were made on the goods he offered, or if the company did not respond in bidding, stamped him as one of the baser sort of vulgarians.

Sales of this description were going on in every direction, and the street rang with the stentorian voices of the sellers. Many of these were mock auctions, as an observer of any intelligence would detect, and as I ascertained beyond doubt almost directly after leaving this man's stand; for, stepping into an open store close at hand, of which there are ranges on either side of the street, a sale of jewellery and watches was going on. A case of jewellery, containing, among other things, a gold watch and chain, apparently of exquisite workmanship, was put up just as I entered, and was started at six cents per article. Bid after bid succeeded, until, at last, the lot was knocked down to a southern gentleman present at fifty cents per item. On making the purchase, he naturally wished to know how many articles the box contained. This information, on the plea that it would delay the sale, was withheld. The auctioneer, however, insisted on the payment of a deposit of fifty dollars, in compliance with the published conditions of the sale, which sum, after a demur on the part of the purchaser, was paid. I could see, however, that he was now sensible he had been duped, and I afterwards learnt that some forty or fifty articles, of almost every fancy description, many of them worthless, such as pins, knives, tweezers, and a variety of other knick-knacks, were artfully concealed from view, by means of a false bottom to the case; this being lifted up revealed the truth. The man was greatly enraged on finding he had been cheated, but was treated with the most audacious coolness, and after some altercation left the store, as he said, to seek redress elsewhere, but I have no doubt he went off with the intention of losing his deposit.

This occurrence put me on my guard, and made me very wary of buying articles at such auctions during my stay in New York, although the apparent beauty and cheapness of many of the articles I saw offered, especially of French manufacture, were sufficient to decoy the most wary, and I did not wonder at people being victimized at such places. Emigrants are the chief sufferers, I was told, by such transactions, from their want of caution, and ignorance of the arts of the accomplished deceivers who conduct them.

Proceeding up Wall-street in the direction of Broadway, I reached that portion of it frequented by stock and real-estate brokers. Here crowds of gentlemanly-looking men, dressed mostly in black, and of busy mien, crowded the thoroughfare with scrip in hand. Each appeared intensely absorbed in business, and as I gazed on the assemblage, I could discover unmistakable symptoms of great excitement and mental anxiety, the proportion of rueful countenances being much greater than is usually seen in similar places of resort in England; a sudden depression in the market at the time might, however, account for much of this, although it is well known that brokers and speculators on the American continent engage in the pursuit with the avidity of professed gamblers.

Hundreds of Negroes were hurrying to and fro through the streets, these were chiefly labourers, decently dressed, and employed either as draymen or porters. They looked happier than labourers in England; and, being bathed in a profuse perspiration from the heat of the weather, their faces shone almost like black satin or patent leather.

After a few days' rest at my boarding-house, to which I was recommended by a touter, and which was in Canal-street, and was kept by a "cute" Down-easter, or native of the New England States, with whom I engaged for bed and board for eight dollars per week, I sallied forth to make my intended observations, preparatory to leaving for the west. Everything wore a novel aspect. The number of foreigners seen in the thoroughfares, the tawdry flimsily-built carriages, which strangely contrast with the more substantial ones seen in England, and the dresses of the people, all seemed strange to me. The habiliments of one or two in particular rivetted my attention. The first was a Kentuckian, who was dressed in a suit of grey home-spun cloth, and wore on his head a fantastical cap, formed of a racoon-skin, beautifully striped, the ears projecting just above his forehead on each side, while the forefeet of the animal, decorated with red cloth, formed the ear-laps, and the tail depended over his back like a quieu, producing a ludicrous effect. His appearance as he passed along attracted little notice, such vagaries being common in America. My attention was also arrested by a person who was arrayed in a hunting suit of buck-skin, curiously wrought with strips of dyed porcupine-quill, and who wore an otter-skin cap and Indian moccasins. There, is, however, little novelty in this costume, which I frequently saw afterwards. Caps of the description I have mentioned are commonly worn in the interior. I subsequently donned one myself, and found it an admirable adjunct to easy travelling.

During my stay at New York, I found the heat almost overpowering, the Indian summer (as the period between autumn and winter is there termed) having set in. An umbrella was quite a necessary appendage at times, to avoid its effects, which are often fatal to Europeans at the time of the summer solstice.

In perambulating the city of New York, its appearance is prepossessing to a visitor; the streets are well laid out, and are wide and regular, the houses being for the most part of the better class. The white or red paint (the latter predominates), and the green and white jalousie, venetian, and siesta blinds, giving a picturesqueness to the scene. Handsome mats lie outside the doors of many of the better description of houses.

Broadway is the principal place of attraction in New York, but it has so often been described by visitors, that it is a work of supererogation to comment much upon it here; as, however, every tourist can see and describe differently the same objects, I must not pass it in silence, especially as it ranks in the view of the New Yorkers, something as Bond-street and Regent-street do in the metropolis of England. It is, however, far inferior to these; it is not one, but a continuous line of streets, and, including Canal-street, extends about three miles in length. The Haarlem Railway comes down a considerable portion of the upper part, the rails being laid in the centre of the street The lower end of Broadway merges into the Battery Park, which is situated at the water's edge. In Broadway are to be seen magnificent hotels, theatres, magazines-de-mode, and all the etceteras of a fashionable mart, not omitting to mention crowds of elegantly dressed ladies and exquisitely attired gentlemen, including many of colour; the latter appearing in the extreme of the fashion, with a redundancy of jewellery which, contrasting with their sable colour, produces to the eye of a stranger an unseemly effect. The shops and stores are fitted up in the Parisian style, appear well attended by customers, and are crowded with the choicest description of goods.

Astor's Hotel, built by the so-called millionaire of that name, is a large but rather heavy-looking pile of building, and forms a conspicuous object in the park. Here many of the elite from the provinces sojourn on visiting the city. The accommodations are stated to be of the first order, and, from a cursory inspection, I should imagine this to be true, the only drawback being the enormous prices charged, exceeding, I was told, the ordinary run of first-class houses of that description. Noticing from the opposite side of the street that the entrance was much crowded, curiosity led me to cross over and ascend the steps and listen to what was going on, supposing it some political demonstration; in this, however, I was mistaken, for I found that the cause of the commotion was the recent arrival and presence of the

celebrated statesman and lawyer, Daniel Webster, **en route** to Washington, whither he was called by Congressional duties. I pressed forward to shake hands with
this great expounder of American laws, as he is called by the citizens, who seemed,
by the way, on the occasion I refer to, to regard him as a sort of divinity. I could
not, however, succeed in getting near enough to accomplish my object, although I
strove hard for it. It was quite amusing to see the anxiety shown by some of those
present to effect the same purpose. The senator kept shaking hands with all around,
repeating over and over again, "Glad to see you, citizens, glad to see you." Amongst
others, a gentlemanly-dressed negro with a gold-headed cane pressed forward and
held out his hand. There was, however, no chance for him in the throng, for he
was rudely pushed back, and I heard several angry exclamations of disapprobation
from the crowd, at the liberty he had taken, one individual in particular crying out,
"Kick that nigger off, what has he to do here." These exclamations caught the ear of
the negro gentleman, and he shrunk back in an instant, as if electrified. Mr. Webster was a yeoman-like looking person, of rather a muscular-build, and at one time
of life was, no doubt, as I have heard, possessed of great physical powers; he had a
heavy and rather downcast turn of features, which were not improved by a pair of
enormous black eyebrows; there was, however, an expression in his physiognomy
that indicated deep thought, and a degree of intelligence above the mediocrity. In
addition to this, there was also a pleasing urbanity in his manner that was certainly contrary to what might have been expected from his personal appearance and
known burly character in business. He gradually retreated up the steps towards the
interior of the hotel, the excessive attentions paid by the crowd appearing trouble-
some to him. He was closely followed, however, by his admirers, whose boisterous
behaviour savoured much more of enthusiasm than deference or politeness. I had
heard that the Americans profess never to do things by halves, and so set this instance down as a proof of their propensity to "go the whole hog," as they are wont
to term their extremes and eccentricities.

The Town-hall, situate at the base of the Park, which is a triangular piece of
land, well laid out and neatly kept, is a light edifice of some taste and architectural
merit, its chief attraction being the white marble of which it is constructed, and
which is brought from the quarries at Sing-Sing, some miles up the river Hudson.
The effect, however, is not good; its exposure to the elements having given it a

blurred or chalky appearance. It is surmounted by a small but elevated cupola, constructed of wood, which some time ago, I was informed by a citizen, caught fire at a pyrotechnic exhibition, and endangered the whole edifice, since which, displays of fire-works have been prohibited in the Park by the civic authorities. At the entrance there is a spacious vestibule, but this, as well as the interior, though elegant in its simplicity of style, is meagre of ornament. Proceeding to the interior, I reached the criminal court, where a squalid-looking prisoner was undergoing trial for murder. The judges and officers of the court were almost entirely without insignia of office, and the counsel employed, I thought, evinced much tact in their proceedings, especially in the cross-examination of witnesses, although they manifested great acerbity of feeling towards each other, and their acrimonious remarks would not, I imagine, have been allowed to pass without remonstrance in an English court of justice. I was told by a by-stander, with whom I entered into conversation, that if found guilty, the prisoner would be conducted to an underground apartment used for the purpose, and privately executed, the law of the State of New York, from motives that ought to be appreciated in England, prohibiting public executions. It is also customary there to allow criminals more time than in England, to prepare for the awful change they are doomed to undergo.

I was informed by a friend that there are some very astute lawyers in America, and I subsequently had opportunities to test the accuracy of the remark. Their code, however, differs materially from the English, although professing to be based upon its principles; and has the preeminent advantage of being pretty free from the intricacies and incongruities that so often tend to defeat justice in the mother-country, and render proceedings at law so expensive and perplexing. The slave laws (called the "codenoir"), adapted for the Southern States, must, however, be excepted, for it is notorious, that to subserve the ends of interested parties, they have been framed so as to present what may with propriety be termed a concatenation of entanglement and injustice to the slave subjects; the very wording of many of these enactments, carrying unmistakable evidence of their being concocted for the almost sole protection of the slave-owners.

Adjoining the Town-hall, or separated only by an avenue, is a heavy, monastic-looking building, used as a bridewell, and called the City Penitentiary. Having remained a considerable time in the hall where the trial was going on, the ago-

nized state of the prisoner and sickening details of the murder caused a disinclina-
tion for the present to continue my perambulations, so I stepped into the Cafe de
l'Independence, in Broadway, and called for a port-wine sangaree, endeavouring,
while I sipped it, smoked a cigar, and read the ***Courier and Inquirer***, to forget the
scene I had just witnessed. Leaving soon after, I pursued my way down Broadway,
passing Peel's Museum and the Astor House, to the Battery Marine Promenade.
This is a delightful spot, the finest in point of situation (although not in extent) of
the kind I ever saw, the Esplanade at Charleston in South Carolina, of which I shall
have by-and-by to speak more particularly, being excepted.

Ladies and gentlemen were promenading up and down, under the umbrageous
foliage of the lofty trees which skirt the Battery Park, and which were as yet un-
scathed by the recent frosts, forming a delightful retreat from the scorching rays
of an American sun. The sea view from this point, with the adjacent scenery, is
interesting and attractive; the broad expanse of ocean in the distance, the highlands
looming in the perspective, the numerous aquatic birds skimming the surface of the
estuary, and the picturesque fort and woody shores of New Jersey, all tending to
diversify the scene and add to its natural beauty. I afterwards visited this place over
and over again, and every succeeding visit added to my admiration and enhanced
its attractions. To the left lies, in panoramic grandeur, the harbour, literally teeming
with ships of all sizes and all nations; while, on the right, the entrance of the majestic Hudson or north river, with crowds of magnificent steamers, traders to Troy,
Albany, and the West, forms a prominent feature in that direction. The passing and
repassing of steamers and other vessels of home-traffic, and the more exciting arrival of ships from foreign parts, give a zest to the scene which must be witnessed
to be fully appreciated.

A day or two after, having obtained, through a friend, leave of admission, I
crossed over to Brooklyn, and visited the Navy-yard. The docks of this establishment contained, at this time, many specimens of American naval architecture of
choice description; amongst the rest, a frigate and several other ships of war lying
in ordinary. Everything appeared to indicate good management and efficiency, as
far as a landsman could judge. This was very discernible on board the vessels we
were allowed to inspect, where the utmost order and cleanliness prevailed. The
officers, I thought, seemed to exact great deference from the men, and their mar-

tinet bearing ill accorded with a republican service, being decidedly more marked than on board British ships of war which I had visited at Deptford, Chatham, and elsewhere in England. Probably a stricter discipline may be found necessary, on account of the equality that exists in America, which might operate to render those under command more difficult of control, if such independence were allowed to be manifested.

I found that the army and navy, in America, are chiefly manned by English, Dutch and Irish, not a few Poles being in the ranks of the former: these are impelled, through lack of employment, and the additional inducement of a tolerably liberal pay, to join the service. The Americans themselves are too sensible of the inconveniences attending public services, as well as too acute, to follow such occupations in time of peace, though when danger has threatened, they have always shown themselves at the instant service of the State, and as citizen soldiers are not, perhaps, to be equalled in any other country.

From the Navy-yard I proceeded to Hoboken; this is a place of great resort in fine weather, and is situate nearly opposite the city of New York, or rather the eastern part of it. Here I found assembled a large company of pleasure-seekers in holiday attire, some lounging under the trees, others in groups at pic-nic, and not a small proportion of the gentlemen regaling themselves at the refreshment stalls or temporary cafes, erected on the grounds, on mint juleps and iced sangarees. The grounds are interspersed with park, woodland, and forest scenery, and are kept in admirable order, the managers studying to maintain the appearance of original nature, and to impress on the mind of the visitor, that he is ruralizing, far from city life, amongst primeval forest shades; the contiguous scenery is not, however, calculated to carry out the idea. It is quite the custom for American husbands to leave their families for the day, and enjoy relaxation in their own way, a practice that I apprehend would not be sanctioned by our English ladies, any more than it would be resorted to by English gentlemen, from motives of kindly and very proper feeling. Here, in a retired spot, is the duelling ground, which has attained no little notoriety in that latitude, as the spot where many a knotty point has been quietly solved by the aid of a pair of pistols or Colt's rifles; although, for the credit of the citizens of New York and its neighbourhood, it must be recorded that they are not so ready to fly to this disgraceful alternative as their ensanguined brethren in the

Southern or Slave States.

My stay in New York being limited by previous arrangements, I was anxious to get back to the city, although a day might well be taken up in ruralizing, and exploring the Arcadian beauties of Hoboken, the favourite resort of the citizens of New York. So, after a pretty general though cursory survey of its attractions, I re-crossed, as I had come, in a ferry propelled by steam. The construction of this boat, a whole fleet of which description were busily plying to and fro, being unique, and unlike any I had seen before, I must not pass it over without remark. In principle it consisted of two barge-like vessels placed side by side, a platform being laid on the top, for the engine, passengers, and steersman; the latter, as in all American steam-vessels, of whatever size, being perched in an elevated round-house on deck. The stem and stern of this vessel were alike, the necessity of turning being thus altogether obviated, as in some of the steam-boats on the Thames.

A practice prevails amongst newspaper publishers in America, which is, I believe, only resorted to in England in cases of public emergency or unusual excitement, and that but seldom; I mean that of posting on large placards the latest arrival of news, home or foreign: thus, whenever you return home after a sojourn in the city, the eager inquiry is sure to be, "Any news up town?" This custom keeps up a lively interest in passing events, and disseminates amongst the citizens at large, the current news of the day, and if it has no other beneficial effects, prevents rumours, that commonly circulate in times of public excitement to the detriment often of many individuals in crowded communities. I noticed the walls of New York thickly posted with placards chiefly of an inflammatory political character. Many of these breathed agrarian principles, that would in Europe have been inadmissible, and would, without doubt, have led to the immediate arrest and imprisonment of the authors. Here, however, they are but little noticed by the populace, and not at all, I believe, by the authorities. Cheap newspapers are pushed into the face of the passer-by, at the corner of every principal thoroughfare, the prices varying from two to six cents. These, as may be supposed, contain, together with the current news, every description of scandal and trash imaginable, their personality being highly offensive, injurious, and reprehensible. Thus the freedom of the press is abused in every part of America, and this powerful engine of "good or ill" converted from a benefit (as it is if managed with propriety) into a public nuisance.

One peculiarity, exceedingly annoying to an Englishman, which is observable even in good society in New York and elsewhere in America, is a prying curiosity as to the affairs of those with whom they converse. Their habits at table also often fill one with disgust, and the want of good-breeding I witnessed on more than one occasion would have been resented in England. This is the more remarkable, as the Americans entertain high notions of refinement, and yet, paradoxical as it may appear, seem to glory in their contempt of good manners. I do not, however, include the ladies in this remark; on the contrary, I must unequivocally assert, that I always observed in them, not only in New York, but in every other part of the North American continent which I visited, the greatest disposition to cover the misdoings of the opposite sex, and a great degree of cultivation and politeness; although they are perfectly freezing in their manners before formal introduction, I do not doubt that there are many among them of great refinement and powers of intellect, their personal appearance being also consonant with their known amiability.

The bustle and drive in the trading quarters of the city is very great. The merchants and their assistants have a hurried manner of doing business, discernible in a moment to a stranger, which is much to be deprecated, and too often leads, as I afterwards found, to disastrous results. Business with these men is in general quite a "go-a-head" sort of affair, and not being accompanied with method, in many cases leads to an embarrassed state of circumstances. Thus it frequently happens, that on investigation, the assets of a merchant who has stopped payment and is a supposed bankrupt, realize more than enough to pay the creditors, and the party finds to his agreeable surprise, that his position is not so bad after all.

The churches and other places of public worship in New York have a temporary appearance, the steeples of the former being, when I visited the city, chiefly of painted-wood. This, I believe, is partly the reason why bells are not used, although a friend in whose presence I noticed this, stated that contempt for so English a custom had much to do with their disuse. If so, the prejudice is not confined to New York alone, for I was not cheered by the inspiriting sound of a peal in any other part of the Union I visited, although I think I have heard they are in use in Philadelphia and some of the eastern cities.

The time I had allotted to remain in New York having expired, and being anxious to proceed on my route before the close of navigation, I reluctantly bade adieu to my kind friends in that city, and made preparations to pursue my way to the more western part of the Union, hoping to reach the Mississippi country before the season when the rivers and canals leading to it would be locked up in ice.

CHAPTER II.

"See how yon flaming herald treads
The ridged and rolling waves,
As, crashing o'er their crested heads,
She bows her surly slaves;
With foam before and fire behind,
She rends the clinging sea,
That flies before the roaring wind,
Beneath her hissing lea."
HOLMES--The Steam Boat.

My first stage, in proceeding to the interior of the country, was to Albany, 160 miles north of New York. To effect this, I took passage, on board a splendidly-equipped steamer, called the *Narraganset*, and esteemed at the time the swiftest boat on the Hudson River. I must confess I was rather timid when I did so, for the reckless manner in which the crack boats are run, in order to maintain their character for celerity, is proverbial, and, as may be supposed, is little consonant with safe travelling. The almost constant recurrence of steam-boat explosions and consequent sacrifice of life, reports of which are daily to be seen in the newspapers, weighed somewhat heavily on my mind, and the latent fear was not lessened by seeing four barrels of pitch rolled on board, the very moment I set foot on the deck of the *Narraganset*. I had to console myself, however, as I best could under the circumstances, and trust to Providence; but had it not been for the payment of my fare, which had previously been arranged, and its inevitable loss if I stopped behind, I believe I should have declined the passage, from my horror of a race. Although, before the boat got under weigh, my lurking fears of explosion were great, they were much enhanced just after starting, in consequence of an opposition boat being loosed from her moorings at the same minute that our vessel got clear of the levee. This accounted for the barrels of pitch I had seen on deck, the heads of which were knocked out just as we entered the Hudson, and a portion of the contents thrown with the fuel into the roaring furnaces; this powerful generator of caloric of course gave increased rapidity to the motion of the engines, and in a couple of hours we left our opponent far behind.

It is remarkable that, although the Americans, as a people, travel more, perhaps, than any other nation, so little attention is paid by them to safety in transit. It is openly avowed that nothing is more common than steam-boat explosions and steam disasters of various kinds throughout this vast continent; and where boats are constructed to carry 1000 or 1200 passengers, as is usual on the American rivers, the loss of life, in case of accident, is fearful to contemplate. I am aware that the subject has been discussed in Congress, and that the question of remedial measures has occupied the attention of the Executive during several successive Presidentships; but still the evil remains, and the public mind in America is almost daily agitated by disasters of this nature. As long as the rampant spirit of competition and desire to outvie their fellows, which prevails amongst a large class of Americans, is tacitly, if not openly, encouraged by the governing powers, such a state of things must exist, and will probably increase; but it is a positive disgrace to a country possessing great natural attractions, and, on this account, visited by many foreigners, that they should by this system be exposed to daily peril of their lives. The acts of Congress lately promulgated, although apparently stringent, are virtually a dead letter, in consequence of the facilities for evasion, and the ingenuity of the offenders. The effort to outrun a rival is attended by an insane excitement, too often participated in by the passengers, who forget for the time that they are in a similar situation to a man sitting on a barrel of gunpowder within a few feet of a raging furnace. I frequently found myself in such a position, in consequence of this dangerous propensity, and the remedy suggested to my mind, and which I recommend to others, was never to take a passage, on American waters, in a first-class steam-boat, as the principle acted upon is to maintain the character of a first-rater at all hazards, regardless of the life or limbs of the helpless passengers.

The ***Narraganset***, like most of the large river steamers, was constructed with three decks, and fitted up in sumptuous style. One large saloon, with a portion partitioned off for the ladies, serving as a cabin and dining apartment. There is no professed distinction of class in the passengers on board steam-boats in America. I found, however, that the higher grades, doubtless from the same causes that operate in other parts of the world, kept aloof from those beneath them.

The scene from the upper or hurricane deck (as it is called) was very attractive. Flowing, as the river Hudson does, through a fine mountainous country, the magnificent scenery on the banks strikes the observer with feelings allied to awe. The stream being broad and tortuous, beetling crags, high mountains and bluffs, and dense forests, burst suddenly and unexpectedly into view; fearful precipices abound here and there, amidst luxuriant groves and uncouth pine barrens, forming altogether a diversity that gives the whole the character of a stupendous panorama.

Before we were out of the tide, which for miles flows up the river, our vessel grounded three times, but after puffing and straining for a considerable time, she got off without damage and pursued her onward course. Most of my fellow-voyagers were disposed to be distant and taciturn, and so I enjoyed the grandeurs of the scene in solitary musings, to which the steamers, sloops under sail, and other vessels proceeding up and down the river, gave a pleasant enlivenment. The promenade deck, crowded with lady passengers and beautiful children, under a gay awning, added to the cheerfulness of the surrounding aspect, and the fineness of the weather, but for the fear of collapsing boilers, would have made the trip one of great enjoyment.

Another drawback I had nearly forgotten, and as it serves to illustrate steam-boat and indeed all other travelling inconveniences in America, I must not pass it over; I refer to the vulgarity of the men passengers, who, in default of better occupation, chew tobacco incessantly, and, to the great annoyance of those who do not practise the vandalism, eject the impregnated saliva over everything under foot. The deck of the vessel was much defaced by the noxious stains; and even in converse with ladies the unmannerly fellows expectorated without sense of decency. The ladies, however, seemed not to regard it, and one bright-eyed houri I saw looking into the face of a long sallow-visaged young man, who had the juice oozing out at each angle of his mouth with disgusting effect, so that enunciation was difficult.

Some miles up the Hudson, on a high piece of table-land, amidst romantic scenery, stands in prominent relief the military college of West Point. It commands an extensive view, and, was, I believe, an important outpost during the late war.

The young graduates were exercising in parties on the parade ground under officers, and appeared dressed in dark jackets with silver-coloured buttons, and light blue trowsers. We saw the targets used by the graduates in artillery, who practise on the river banks; at least, it was so stated by a fellow-passenger, who either was, or pretended to be, acquainted with all the affairs of that college.

Beneath the summit of a high bluff, covered with wood, contiguous to the college, I observed a monument or obelisk, which I ascertained to have been erected to the memory of Kosciusko, a Polish patriot, who took a prominent part in the annihilation of British rule in America. It had a very picturesque effect, and was regarded with feelings of veneration by many of the American passengers, one of whom paid a tribute to the departed hero, which he wound up by observing with nasal emphasis and lugubrious countenance, "If twarnt for that ere man, wher'd we be, I waunt to know; not here I guess." This sentiment, although I could scarcely see the point of it myself, elicited half-a-dozen "do tells" and "I waunt to knows" from those around; expressions which, foolish as they sound to English ears, are in common use in the northern and eastern states, when an individual acquiesces in, or is anxious to know more about, what is stated.

As the scenery on the Hudson, although picturesque and highly romantic, savours somewhat of sameness, I shall forbear any further description of it. No one visiting America should omit, if possible, a passage to Albany, in order to enjoy, perhaps, the finest natural scenery in the world.

The individual who delivered the eulogium I have noted on Kosciusko, stated, that at the time of the war, an immense chain cable was thrown across the river at West Point, to prevent the British vessels proceeding to the interior, and this they in vain tried to destroy by firing chain or bar shots.

After a favourable passage, we at length reached Albany, which is an extensive city, and the depot for produce, especially wheat, brought *via* the Erie Canal from the interior; being, in fact, the storehouse of the trade to and from the interior States of the Union, west, as well as from Canada and the Lakes. It is finely situated on the west bank of the Hudson; many of its inhabitants are descended from the first colonists, especially the adventurous and persevering Dutch, who, like the Scotch, cling with tenacity to the spot they fix upon, and quickly accumulate property. This city is continually growing in importance, from the vast number of small capitalists who flock there and settle; and it will eventually, no doubt, vie with New York itself in wealth and importance. As I determined to make no stay here, but to proceed up the Erie Canal to Buffalo, I did not see much of this place, and must therefore omit any lengthened description of it. From what I did see, it appeared a densely-populated, well-built city, laid out with much regularity, and boasting of many substantial buildings, several of the edifices being constructed of white marble.

Having secured a passage on board a canal packet about to start, I at once embarked, and in a few hours after was running up the Erie Canal at the rate of six miles an hour, the boat being towed by four light horses of high mettle. The trappings of these animals were of a novel description, bells being appended to various parts of the harness, and streamers, or plumes of white hair and gaudy ribbons, floating in the air from the bridle of each. A postilion, in a suit of grey, with an otter-skin cap, rode on the rearmost or saddle horse, and his *nonchalance* and perfect command of his team were surprising. This boat was some sixty yards in length, and constructed only for passengers and their luggage. The interior formed a long saloon in miniature, fitted up with lounges, and tastefully decorated; a promenade on the deck or top furnishing a good place for exercise. At night our saloon was converted into a general dormitory, a portion being partitioned off for the ladies, by ranges of shelves being suspended from the sides, on which were laid the mattresses, &c. Owing to the number of locks and stoppages at the miserable towns and villages on the canal banks, our passage to Buffalo took several days; and the country being flat and uninteresting, although divided into farms, which in general appeared to be in a state of tolerable cultivation, I was not a little relieved when we began to approach the city.

The formation of the Erie Canal was one of those grand internal improvements frequently to be met with in that country, and which have contributed to its general prosperity in no small degree. The projector of this vast undertaking, De Witt Clinton, is justly esteemed by American citizens, who regard him as a public benefactor, and his name ranks with the founders of their independence. The canal runs, for a considerable distance before it reaches Buffalo, parallel with the lake, but separated from it by a sort of artificial sea-wall. As we merged into the vicinity of this magnificent inland sea, the sun was shining brightly, and gave it the appearance of molten silver. As far as the eye could reach, a wide expanse of water presented itself, and the distant shores of Canada gave beauty to the scene. At Black-rock we could distinguish the sites of the British fortifications, from which in the last war red-hot cannon-balls were ejected, to the dismay of the terrified Americans, and the destruction of many of their houses.

Buffalo is a flourishing city on the border of Lake Erie, and about twenty miles south of the Falls of Niagara. It is within the boundary of the state of New York, and has of late years greatly increased in extent, wealth, and population. The old town, quite an inconsiderable place, on the site of which the present city has risen, phoenix-like, was burnt to the ground during the late war, by some British officers, who made a sortie from the Canada shores; which circumstance, having been handed down from father to son, still rankles in the bosoms of many of the older inhabitants, who do not fail to state their belief that retributive justice will eventually be administered by the entire subjugation of Canada. During my rather prolonged stay in Buffalo, I had frequent opportunities of discovering that the most rancorous feelings exist on the subject; and in proof of this it may be remembered by the reader that the Canadian insurgents were assisted at the late insurrection by supplies of stores from this city. These were conveyed to Navy Island by the steamer *Caroline*, which was subsequently seized, and sent over the Falls of Niagara by the British troops, a number of the crew being cruelly massacred.

From inquiries made of parties well informed on the subject, both in Canada and the United States, I am convinced that the public act of Sir John Colborne, before quitting the governorship of the province, in 1835, viz., the allotment or appropriation of 346,252 acres of the soil, as a clergy reserve, and the institution of the fifty-seven rectories, was the chief predisposing cause of the insurrection. By this Act a certain portion of land in every township was set apart for the maintenance of "a Protestant clergy," under which ambiguous term, the clergy of the Church of England have always claimed the sole enjoyment of the funds arising from the sale of such portions of land. This is looked upon by dissenters of all denominations as a direct infringement of the original intention of the Act, which they maintain was for the purpose of aiding the Protestant cause at large against the innovations of the Roman Catholic Church. Much ill-will and sectarian prejudice are the natural consequence; in fact, the Act is a perfect apple of discord throughout the Canadas, and has engendered more animosity and resentment than any one legislative act, sanctioned by the Home Government, since the acquisition (if so it can he called) of the country. It is an indelible disgrace to England, that such a manifestly bigoted and narrow-minded policy should have been allowed to continue so long; and I am fully persuaded that this enactment, which, there is little doubt, originated in sectarianism, perpetuates a degree of rancorous feeling in the minds of people there, that is sufficient to account for the disaffection and tendency to rebellion that ever and anon displays itself; and that to remove this blister, and allow the application of these funds to all creeds alike, would be to restore peace, and convert doubtfully-affected communities to allegiance. If there is one consideration that ought to weigh in the minds of the British as a people, to endeavour to rivet the affections of the Canadians, more than another, and prevent the ultimate cession of that country to the Americans, it is, that the dependency affords now the only asylum for those persecuted outcasts of humanity, the slaves of the United States. Canada, the land of freedom, is associated in their minds with paradisaical thoughts of happiness--and many a heart-stricken creature in the Southern States of America, as I had many opportunities of ascertaining, toils on in content, with "Canada" in view, as the ultimatum of his hopes and the land of his redemption.

The population of Buffalo is fluctuating, owing to the vast number of emigrants who are constantly arriving, **en route** to Ohio, Michigan, and the far West. It averages in population, about ten thousand. The city is not of great extent, and consists in chief of one principal thoroughfare, called Maine-street, which is wide, the lower part terminating at the water's edge, along which spacious stores are erected for the reception of wheat and goods in transit. The harbour is formed by an arm of Lake Erie uniting with Buffalo river. Here are always congregated a large fleet of steamers, many of them of leviathan dimensions, which are employed in running to and from Detroit, in Michigan, and the intermediate ports, as well as in the Upper Lake trade. Being quite a depot, Buffalo bids fair, ere the lapse of many years, to be the grand emporium of the West. The public buildings do not deserve much notice; the Eagle Theatre, a joint-stock concern, being the only building of much interest. There are, however, several spacious hotels, and two or three banks, that boast some architectural merit, although much, I believe, cannot be said as to their stability. The lateral streets are rather obscure, and, not being regularly built upon, give the city an unfinished look. These are, however, dotted here and there with chateaux, having good gardens well arranged. The Niagara Railway station is situated to the left of Maine-street, about half-way up that premier thoroughfare.

At night the distant moan of the Niagara falls was audible, and this, together with what I had heard and read, made me very anxious to visit the spot. Accordingly, one splendid morning I started by train for the purpose. For some miles before we reached Niagara, we constantly heard the roar of the rushing waters, and were thus prepared for the stupendous scene that burst upon the view, as we alighted at the doors of that *ne plus ultra* of modern hostelries, the Pavilion Hotel.

My powers of description will fall short of conveying to the mind of the reader the awful grandeur of this cataract, so often commented upon by travellers. The first impression felt by me was, that the whole substratum on which I stood, which seemed to tremble, was about to be swept away by the vast inundation. It was not the height of the falls, but the immense body of water, which comprehends, with constant accumulations from the tributaries on the way, the overflowings of Lakes Erie, Superior, Michigan, and Huron. The astonishing effect of such a body of water, dashed abruptly over a precipice of 150 perpendicular feet, may be conceived; such is the momentum of this immense volume of fluid, that, when it strikes the rocky bed at the base of the cataract, it rebounds in a thick cloud of vapour--and when the sun's rays intercept it, as was the case when I arrived there, a beautiful rainbow of vivid colours encircles the area of the chasm, and, together with the natural curiosities and situation of the entire scene, presents to the amazed beholder, the effect of a highly-executed picture in a frame of sun-light, although far surpassing the productions of human skill, which may well be said, in comparison, to sink into utter insignificance.

A large company of visitors were assembled at the time of my arrival, probably from all parts of the world--so that I found it impossible to get a bed, unless I penetrated into the interior with a view to obtain accommodation at some farm-house, or crossed to the Canada side; but, feeling too tired, after the day's excitement, to pursue either such course, I took an evening train and returned to Buffalo the same day, where I arrived at 9 P.M.

About three miles from Buffalo is an Indian village, called Tonawanda. I frequently saw parties of the inhabitants, who resort to the city to dispose of their wares and produce. Some of the warriors were fine athletic fellows, of great stature, the lowest I saw being over six feet in height. They were clothed in tanned buck-skin, curiously fringed and ornamented with porcupine-quills richly dyed; their squaws (wives) being enveloped in fine Canadian blue broad cloth, their favourite costume; the crimson or other gaudy-coloured selvedge forming a conspicuous ornament.

Like all the aborigines of America, they cling with tenacity to primeval habits and customs, resisting every attempt made by the white population, to make or persuade them to conform to civilized life. The ill-usage they have been subjected to by the Americans, may, however, account for this in a great measure. They were described to me by one of the residents as a dissipated set of fellows, who squandered all they got in "fire-water," as they term ardent spirits, and when inebriated are so quarrelsome that it is dangerous in the highest degree to irritate them.

Not very long after I arrived, a circumstance occurred that threatened most fearful consequences. The Indians whom I have before referred to were in the frequent habit, when they came to the city, to dispose of their produce (for many of them followed husbandry) of getting so tipsy, that there was continual danger of bloodshed; their natural animosity on such occasions being roused with fearful vehemence, so that the authorities were compelled to adopt some steps to remedy the evil. It was no uncommon occurrence to see an Indian waggon by the road-side, with its pair of horses *sans* driver, who might have been found either drunk or quarreling at the other end of the city. And although the horses were always impounded, and a fine inflicted, still the nuisance continued without abatement, in fact, was rather on the increase. The new Mayor, being a man more alive than his predecessor to this evil, caused a regulation to be passed by the Civic Council, that any Indian found so far the worse for liquor in the streets of Buffalo as to be incapable of taking care of himself, should be punished by being made to work on the high roads for a short period, with an iron ball and chain attached to his leg. When this law was promulgated, there was a strong impression that the Indians would show resistance. This was soon found to be a correct view of the case, for not a week had elapsed before two warriors were brought before the Mayor, and sentenced to ten days' probation at road-mending, in pursuance of the decree. They had, however, only been at work two days in the upper part of Maine-street, in charge of two constables, when a large body of their fraternity, armed *cap-a-pie,* entered the city, and, with horrid yells and brandished tomahawks, rescued the culprits, knocked off their chains, and carried them in triumph to the Indian village, amidst fearful threats of fire and blood. As this attack was unexpected, no resistance was offered; and although there was much discussion afterwards, about the laws being vindicated and an example being made, the matter, from motives, no doubt, of public safety, was allowed to drop, and for the future the red men had it all their own way, although there were certainly signs of amendment, and the evil decreased to a very great extent. The Indian maxim being, "Firm in friendship but ruthless in war," there is little doubt that the course pursued on this occasion by the city authorities, was the best under such circumstances.

Lake Erie is a fine piece of water, being 265 miles long, from Buffalo to Detroit, the two extreme ends, and averaging about 60 miles broad. At its north-east end it communicates with Lake Ontario and the Canadian shores, by the gut or strait of Niagara. Towards the west end are numerous islands and banks, which are furnished with light-houses for the guidance of the mariner. Its waters wash the foot of Maine-street (Buffalo) where they meet the river from which that city takes its name. It is frequently visited by furious gales, which play havoc with the steamers, many of which are annually wrecked.

While I remained in Buffalo, I took several excursions to the towns that skirt this beautiful inland sea. On one of these occasions, the steamer was driven by stress of weather to take shelter in the small harbour of Huron, some distance up the lake; this we reached with much difficulty, the violence of the sea threatening every moment the total destruction of the vessel. As we entered the harbour, the air rang with a shout of welcome from the inhabitants of the place, who had been watching our perilous progress in great anxiety, and were assembled at the end of the little pier. Here we remained for two days and nights, the wind blowing all that time with the fury of a hurricane; the lake, during the storm, presenting the appearance of the sea in a stiff north-wester, the white-crested waves rising in violent commotion to a fearful height.

Huron is but a small and uninteresting place, situate in a most unwholesome locality, lying opposite to a murky swamp, whose poisonous vapours spread disease and death around. It is the highway to Sandusky city, an inland border town, rendered famous for the obstinacy with which the inhabitants and a body of U.S.

Infantry defended a fort there against the attacks of the British troops in 1812. Having ascertained the captain's intention not to sail until the day following, and it being described as a very attractive spot, I hired a horse, and, after a seven miles' ride through a country dotted with farm houses, which had a desolate look, and the lands appertaining to which were subdivided by zigzag log fences (hedges being unknown in the back settlements), I reached the so-called city, which is built in nearly the form of a parallelogram, the area of greensward having a pretty effect. Here are some good hotels, and a seminary or college for young ladies, which is much patronized by the better classes of the northern and eastern states, especially New York. I looked in vain for the Fort, which has, since the war, been demolished; but the landlord of the hotel at which I afterwards dined, took me to its site, and related several incidents that occurred in connection with the fortress, and the struggle between the belligerent parties at the time. As, however, I considered these somewhat apocryphal, from several of his relations failing to hang together, and his decided bias against the Britishers, as he called the English, I shall not trouble the reader with the details. After viewing the place and its suburbs to my satisfaction, and after an excellent dinner of green maize and venison, I rode back to the steamer.

It was towards evening when I arrived; and, as I approached Huron, by the banks of the creek that divides the swamp I have mentioned, and which was unusually swollen, I noticed a canoe that had broken loose from its moorings, drifting down the current; a moment afterwards the owner arrived in breathless haste, to endeavour to save it from destruction; his exertions were, however, useless, and, finding there was no alternative, he hailed the bystanders, and offered the reward of a dollar to any one who would swim to and paddle the canoe on shore; this offer was eagerly caught at by a tall man, of great muscular power, who was amongst the crowd, and who at once threw off his coat and plunged into the stream. This was very rapid, and, after a few moments battling with the turbid current, he was overpowered; uttering a loud cry for assistance, which I shall never forget and which rang in my ears like a death knell, he disappeared from the view of the spectators, and, being probably entangled in the trees and debris that were floating down the torrent, he did not rise again. A loud wail arose from the terrified assemblage, who were unable to render the poor fellow any assistance, and who ran about in frantic excitement. The canoe was lost, being carried at a rapid rate into the open lake, where it capsized, and sunk immediately. After dragging for the body for upwards of an hour, it was fished up from under some logs of timber moored some distance below where the catastrophe occurred. The body being landed and placed on the bank, a loud altercation ensued as to the means to be used to attempt resuscitation--a vain hope--but still persisted in by those assembled. Some wanted to roll it on a barrel, others to suspend it by the heels, that the water might be voided. At length a doctor arrived, and, after some inquiry, pronounced effort useless, from the time the body had been under water. This at once damped the ardour of the crowd, although it did not discourage a female, who had taken a prominent part in the operations, and who, with that true womanly tenderness and solicitude which do honour to her sex, and which are nowhere more conspicuous than in America, insisted upon the corpse being taken to a neighbouring house, where, like a ministering angel, she persevered in her efforts for a considerable time, although of course without effect.

The banks of Lake Erie, in the vicinity of Huron, are thickly studded with small trees and coppice wood. This scenery, being interspersed with open natural meadow-land, gives it a park-like aspect, and several spots would, graced with a mansion, have formed an estate any nobleman in Europe might have been proud of, the shores of Canada, looming in the hazy distance, giving a fine effect to the scene.

The noise and disagreeable odour arising from the bull-frogs and other reptiles that infest the swamp opposite the village at night, filled the air, and rendered it impossible for me to sleep. As I lay restless on my bed, I suddenly heard a gun fired, and, starting up in some alarm, I hastily put on my clothes and descended to the bar of the hotel. Here several of the inmates were assembled, and were preparing to cross the creek with lanterns, to explore the swamp, cries of distress having been distinctly heard, as of some benighted traveller who had lost his way. After listening intently, and firing several rifles to guide the wanderer or apprize him that assistance was at hand, the party crossed the creek in a canoe, and moved along the skirts of the morass, hallooing loudly all the time; the cries, however, heard only at intervals at the commencement, became gradually indistinct, and at last ceased altogether. After an ineffectual search for an hour or more, the party again turned towards Huron, strongly impressed with the belief, that the unfortunate being had sunk with his horse in the soft bed of the swamp, which is some miles in extent, and had perished miserably. The day following, I visited the nearest point from which the cries were heard, but I could discern no sign of the sufferer, nor could I even trace footmarks; this, however, is not remarkable, as they would speedily be obliterated by the many reptiles nurtured in the morass. It was afterwards questioned, whether the supposed wanderer was only a catamount, a species of jaguar that emits doleful cries at night.

The storm having abated, I soon after returned on board, and in due course reached Buffalo, where I had the pleasure of meeting with an old acquaintance, from whom I had long been separated, and who had delayed his intended voyage up the lake, to await my return. A large proportion of the population of Buffalo are people of colour, and one quarter of the town is almost exclusively inhabited by them; many of these, I regret to add, are living in a state of degradation pitiable to behold, apparently without the least endeavour being made by their white fellow-citizens to improve their condition. Some of these coloured people keep eating-houses, for the accommodation of those of their own complexion, but the greater number are employed as stokers and steam-boat hands. A few of these men, despite the prejudice that exists (and it is nowhere in the Union more marked than in Buffalo), rise above the common level, and by that probity of character and untiring energy, which I believe to be inherent in the race, become men of substance.

One instance of this deserves especial notice, as the subject of it had, entirely by the good qualities mentioned, amassed a fortune, and had married a woman of English birth. I was introduced to this individual some time after my arrival in Buffalo, and his singularly correct views and uprightness of character made me partial to his company. His wife was a notable, well-informed, good-looking woman, about forty years of age. Irrespective of colour, I certainly admired her discrimination in the choice of a partner, although she was looked down upon by the wives of the white citizens, and, in common with her husband, was almost entirely shunned by them. There may, perhaps, have been a higher consideration than that of a good settlement to cause an English woman in this instance to marry a dark mulatto; but I was always of opinion, and she confirmed this by hints dropped casually, that the consideration of a fortune had more to do with the alliance than love. This gentleman kept a good house, and had many servants. His wife being fond of amusements, he hired a box for her use at the Eagle Theatre, which she always attended alone, the etiquette of the white citizens not permitting his attendance with her. He appeared almost always in a desponding mood, a tendency arising entirely from the insulting demeanour used towards him by the citizens; and he frequently talked of removing to Canada, or the far West, to avoid the treatment he was subjected to at the hands of a pack of young scoundrels, who took every opportunity to annoy and treat him with indignity for marrying a white woman. The consequence was, that neither he nor his wife scarcely ever ventured out. If they did so, it was never in company, and usually after dark. I was politely offered the use of their box at the theatre during my stay, and on one occasion availed myself of the offer. But I never ventured again--the box was evidently marked, and during the performance I was subjected to the most disgusting remarks and behaviour from the audience. Indeed, this was carried so far, that I retired long before the curtain dropped. So intent were his fellow-citizens on annoying this inoffensive man, that soon after he was mobbed in Maine-street by the young desperadoes I have referred to, who, from their determined opposition to intermixed marriages, were known in the place as "anti-amalgamists." On this occasion poor P---- nearly lost his life, and, but for running, would, no doubt, have done so; as it was, he was much burnt about the head and neck, the ruffians in the scuffle having set fire to his frock-coat, which was of linen.

It is rather remarkable that, at St. Louis, on the Missouri, some ten months afterwards, I met this very man, he having purchased some government land in a remote part of that state. Our meeting was quite accidental, for I crossed the street and accosted him as he was hurrying along. In the course of our interview he pressed me earnestly to go up the country with him; but this I declined from motives of prudence, the route lying through a slave-holding state, where a white and coloured man travelling on terms of equality, would be sure to excite suspicion. He had a small bundle of papers under his arm, and on my remarking he appeared intent on business, he stated they were his free papers, and that not ten minutes before he had been challenged to produce them; but this, he said, would not have prevented his arrest and detention in the city gaol until the authorities of Buffalo had been written to under suspicion of his being a fugitive, had he not taken the precaution, before he left that city, to obtain from the mayor a certificate of his intention to proceed to the Missouri country, and the object of his visit. He told me that if he liked his purchase, he should build a house on it, and cultivate the land as a farm, as his continued residence in Buffalo, after the disposition to annoy him shown by the citizens, rendered his stay there out of the question. I afterwards dined with him at his "hotel," which was an obscure tavern in an unfrequented part of the city, in and about which I saw several coloured people. I afterwards ascertained that this was what is there derisively termed a "nigger boarding-house," and that the keepers of superior hotels would not think of accommodating a coloured person even for a night. From subsequent experience in such matters, I have no doubt that this version was a true one.

The hotels and cafes in the Slave States are all frequented by slave owners and dealers; these would not think of putting up at quarters where "coloured folks" were entertained. This distinction is so marked, that no negro would attempt to apply for refreshment at the bar of such places, as the inevitable consequence of such a liberty would be refusal, if not summary ejectment. It is therefore the custom, in all southern towns and cities, for the negro population to resort to places kept expressly for the accommodation of coloured people. These are not always kept by men of their own complexion, but often by white men, who, having become friendly with them, have lost caste with the whites, and are in fact discarded by them.

In the harbour of Buffalo, I saw two brigs, that during the war in 1812 had been captured by the Americans, and sunk somewhere up the lake on the American side. These had recently been raised by means of apparatus invented by an ingenious American. They were strong, substantially-built brigs, of about 250 tons burden each. I was surprised to find what a preserving effect the lake water had upon the timber, the wood being almost black in colour, and so hard that it was difficult to make an impression upon it even with an axe. These vessels had been sold to a shipping company, and were at the time employed, I think, in the Chicago or Upper Lake trade.

I had frequently heard of the number of rattle and other snakes to be met with on the banks of the lake, but these have been nearly exterminated by the settlers. During my stay in the suburbs I only found a few water-snakes, basking in the sun amongst the wilderness of aquatic plants that cover the surface of the water in the creeks.

The superstitious dread of inhaling the east wind blowing from the mouth of the lake, is now exploded, and is considered in the light of a by-gone tale; although, for three-quarters of a century, it was considered baneful even to the healthy. Consumptive patients are, however, soon carried off, the biting blasts from the Canadian shores proving very fatal in pulmonary complaints, and the winters being very severe.

A plentiful supply of excellent fish of various sorts, is procured from the lake. These are salted in barrels, and find a ready market in the northern and eastern states.

My abode in the city of Buffalo extended over the greater part of a year, and during this period I had frequent opportunities of witnessing that tendency to over-reach that has, perhaps, with some justice, been called a disposition in the generality of Americans to defraud. I do not mean to stygmatize any particular class of men in this imputation, but I must record my decided conviction, arising from transactions with them, that business with the mass of citizens there is not that upright system that obtains with such successful results in the mother country, amongst those engaged in commercial relations. Perhaps it would be but fair to make some excuse for men of this class, in a country whose heterogeneous population, and consequent exposure to competition, renders it a struggle to obtain a livelihood. It is notorious that thousands of men in America are obliged, as it were, to succumb to this influence or become paupers, and are thus driven out of the paths of strict rectitude and honesty of purpose, and compelled to resort to all sorts of chicanery to enable them to make two ends meet. In no instance is this more observable than in the "selling" propensities of the Americans. "For sale" seems to be the national motto, and would form an admirable addendum to the inscription displayed on the coins, "E pluribus unum." Everything a man possesses is voluntarily subjected to the law of interchange. The farmer, the land speculator, and the keeper of the meanest grocery or barber's stall, are alike open to "a trade," that is, an exchange of commodities, in the hope or prospect of some profit, honestly or dishonestly, being attached to the transaction. This induces a loose, gambling propensity, which, indulged in to excess, often leads to ruin and involvement, and, if absolute beggary is deferred, causes numerous victims to be perpetually floundering in debt, difficulty, and disgrace.

CHAPTER III.

"Then blame mo not that I should seek, although I know not thee,
To waken in thy heart its chords of holiest sympathy,
It is for woman's bleeding heart, for woman's humbled form,
O'er which the reeking lash is swung, with life's red current warm."
E M CHANDLER

On a fine morning in June, I took my departure from Buffalo, in the lake steamer *Governor Porter*, for the port of Cleveland in the state of Ohio. The sun was shining on the silvery bosom of the lake, which in a dead calm gave it a refulgent glassy appearance. We had not, however, been two hours at sea before the clouds began to collect, and a heavy gale came on with rapidity. This continued to increase until the day following, during which the vessel had passed Cleveland, the place of my destination, and was driving before a furious north-wester towards Detroit, at the head of the lake. The captain stated that all his endeavours to make the landing-place at Cleveland had been unavailing, but if those passengers whom he had engaged to land there would proceed with him on the voyage to his destination, he would land them on his return, which he said would probably be in three or four days. As this offer necessarily included board, the three passengers, who were in the same predicament as myself, after a short consultation agreed to accept it; and as time was not an object to me, I did not demur, for I much wished to have a view of the country in that direction. Had either of us dissented, the captain would, probably, have landed us at the next port, a result that would have involved the expense and inconvenience of a thirty miles' ride, or thereabouts, to Cleveland, in a rough stage, over rougher roads.

The weather moderated towards sunset, and we had a very favourable passage to the head of the lake, and entering Detroit harbour, which lies at the foot of the town, I soon after landed, and took a stroll into it. It is not a very populous place, the inhabitants being, I should say, under 4000. The houses are in general, heavy dirty-looking buildings, though the streets are tolerably wide, and built with regularity. It is, I believe, peopled principally by French and Dutch, who appeared to be in low circumstances, and who follow the usual town occupations.

This town, which is essentially Gaelic in appearance, is situated on the west side of the strait, between Lakes St. Clare and Erie, and is within sight of Malden in Canada, with the shores of which province a constant trade or communication is kept up by steam. Here is situated an extensive government agency for the sale of land in Michigan; whither, at the time, vast numbers of new settlers were daily proceeding in search of homes and happiness. I saw many of these on their way, and as they toiled to their new homes, they looked haggard, forlorn, and abject; and I thought I could distinguish in almost all, especially the women, an aspect of grief that indicated they were exiles, who had left behind all that tended to make life joyous and happy, to seek a precarious existence in an unknown wilderness. As the town afforded few attractions, the only place of amusement being a temporary theatrical exhibition, I was not a little rejoiced when the vessel again started down the lake, which she did with every advantage of favourable weather. In due course we reached Cleveland, and, as I was anxious to proceed onwards, I took but a cursory view of the place, which is, like Detroit, situated on a somewhat rising ground. It appeared a thriving town, and the hotels were in general superbly fitted up.

As I was strolling towards the canal to take my passage to the Ohio river, a little incident occurred, which, as it illustrates a very old adage, I will not omit. Passing some low-built houses near the canal, my attention was arrested by the screams of a female, who uttered loud cries for assistance.

Hastening to the door of the house from which the alarm proceeded, I lifted the latch in great trepidation, when I saw a man just about to strike a woman (who proved to be his wife) with an uplifted chair. The fellow was vociferating loudly, and appeared in a towering passion. My first impulse was to cry out "Drop it!" when, lo! as if I had, like Katerfelto, the by-gone professor of legerdemain, cried "Presto," the scene changed, and both man and woman, who were Americans of the lower class, commenced bullying me in right earnest. I made my retreat with some difficulty, as they seemed, both of them, inclined to serve me roughly for my well-intentioned, though, perhaps, mistimed interference. As I made my escape, however, I intimated, pretty loudly, that I should at once apply to a magistrate on the subject, a threat, by-the-bye, that was little regarded, and only increased the showers of abuse levelled at me. As my appealing to a magistrate would be of little avail in the case of a family jar, and would certainly have entailed inconvenience and delay, I did not carry my threat into execution, wondering, at the same time, at my temerity in interfering in a quarrel between man and wife, which I now practically learnt, for the first time in my life, was to incur the unmitigated anger of both, and to learn how true it is that

"Those who in quarrels interpose,   Must oft expect a bloody nose."

I visited the portion of the town appropriated by the Mormons as a residence. Here, in the midst of their dwellings, they had erected a temple for worship, which, on their emigrating west, their arch-leader, Smith, prophesied would, by the interposition of heaven, be destroyed by fire. The prophecy was verified as to the fact, but heaven had, it appeared, little to do with it; for it was ascertained to be the work of an incendiary of their sect, who was detected and brought to condign punishment.

I was afterwards informed by an American gentleman, to whom I had a letter of introduction, and who had been a great sufferer by these impostors, that some time before the great body of Mormons migrated to the interior, they started a bank. Having managed to put a vast number of their notes in circulation, for which they received produce, they closed the doors, and left the public to be losers by their nefarious schemes. I had the misfortune myself, in my ignorance, to take from a dishonest store-keeper a ten-dollar bill of this spurious currency, and did not detect the imposture until I offered it to the captain of the boat I had engaged a passage in to *La Belle Riviere*, as the Ohio is called. I must mention, however, that I took it previously to the interview with the gentleman I have adverted to, and actually, without knowing it, had the note in my pocket-book when he mentioned the default of these pseudo bankers. I paid ten dollars for a useful lesson.

The passengers from Cleveland formed a motley group; for, irrespective of French, Dutch, Americans, and Canadians, we had on board eight or ten families of the Mormon sect, following in the wake of their leaders, Smith and Rigdon, to their new settlement in the far west. These people were very reserved, and seemed inclined to keep aloof from their fellow-passengers. This, however, may be accounted for by the prejudice so justly existing at the time against them, as a body, from the causes I have already mentioned; in fact, the indignation of the people could hardly be kept in check by the authorities, and lynching was resorted to on more than one occasion. The men were clothed in drab broad-cloth, and wore large white hats; their garb altogether resembling that of the more respectable Society of Friends, in America. The resemblance, however, ceases with the dress, for, if reports speak true, and they are many-tongued, they are very exceptionable in their morality and general principles, amongst other peculiarities, polygamy being allowed, for the avowed purpose of extending and perpetuating the sect.

Our progress was pretty rapid, though it lay through an uninteresting country, in many parts uncultivated and barren-looking. Massillon is a very flourishing town, with some good stores and two or three hotels. As the captain was obliged to make a short stay here, I went into the town and, stepping into an hotel to procure a cigar, I found a company engaged in earnest conversation, interrupted at intervals by loud laughter. On inquiry, I was told that the landlord had that morning been played a Yankee trick by a travelling pedlar, who had stopped the previous night at his house. It appeared that the same man had some months before practised on the landlord; but, either supposing the matter blown over and forgotten, or, what is more likely, with a view to put another of his arts into exercise, he again put up at the same house. The proprietor, however, at once recognized the pedlar, and after taxing him with the cheat he had practised on the former occasion, wound up his lecture by stating, in true American style, that if he again succeeded in cheating him he would forego the amount of his tavern expenses. The man exclaimed, "Done," and at once it appeared set his wits to work to obtain the object. A few hours after the conversation, the fellow brought in from his waggon some boxes of fancy goods, and endeavoured to induce the landlady to purchase. This, however, no doubt prompted by her husband, she resolutely refused, and he had them removed to his room upstairs, as is customary. After breakfast, the following morning, he called the landlady aside and said he forgot the day before to show her a fancy quilt of superior workmanship, and if she would only look at it he would be satisfied, as it was one of great beauty. She consented to this, and the man at once went to his waggon, which was now at the door, he being about to start, and brought in a box which contained, amongst numerous other articles, the quilt he had been eulogizing. The landlady was much taken with its appearance, and after some little persuasion consented to become the purchaser. Accordingly, the bargain was concluded, and the balance between his tavern bill and the article in question was handed over at the hotel bar to the pedlar, who at once started from the house, the landlord on his doing so jocosely remarking on the conversation of the previous day, in reply to which the wily pedlar observed, that "he guessed it was all right." Soon after the man left, the landlady called her spouse to the inner room, and showing him her bargain, said she had been induced to buy the quilt, because it was an exact match for the one in the large room up-stairs. This led to a female help (as servants are there called), being despatched to the room to fetch and compare the original with that newly purchased. The girl speedily returned in the greatest consternation, saying it had vanished. The truth now became apparent; the artful pedlar had actually sold the landlady her own quilt!

This ludicrous circumstance led to the confusion I had noticed when I arrived; the man had gone they knew not whither, and had it been possible to overtake him, I question whether he would have been pursued, the cleverness of the trick being highly applauded by the company, and the landlord feeling, perhaps, ashamed of being outwitted a second time, after himself giving the challenge. The ingenuity of American pedlars in cozening their countrymen, has long been proverbial, and in general, people are wary of them; they have, however, I suppose by long practice, become such adepts at roguery, that however alive to their propensities, folks are daily victimized by such men. It was nothing new to hear a roguish action applauded, but on this occasion the company were vociferous in his praise, and declared they would certainly patronize him when he came that way again, for he deserved encouragement.

After strolling through the town, which presented little worth recording, I again returned to the boat, which proceeded on its way. I had frequently heard and read of those vast flocks of wild pigeons which periodically pursue their flight to milder latitudes: and, as the boat was now approaching the centre of the state of Ohio, where myriads of these birds were seen the year before, I anxiously watched the horizon for their appearance. For several days, however, I was doomed to disappointment, and gave it up in despair; but a day or two after, when in the vicinity of the Tuscarawas river, it being about noon, the helmsman suddenly called out, "A field of pigeons." This announcement called all hands to the promenade deck of the packet. Looking in the direction indicated, a heavy black cloud appeared in the far horizon; this seemed to extend from right to left, and was so dense that the novices amongst us at once pronounced it, either a mistake or a hoax. The helmsman declared that it was neither, and that we should soon be convinced of it. The cloud seemed now gradually and visibly to spread; in truth, the whole firmament in that direction was totally obscured. By this time a general rummage had commenced in the boat for fire-arms; the captain hailed the driver on the towing path, who pulled up, and the boat was moored by the canal side. We now landed, intending to replenish the larder of the vessel with what, to most of the passengers, was a rare treat. On the left bank of the canal, and on the banks of the river, which here ran parallel with it, was a forest of gigantic trees; and, as the birds were evidently making in that direction, it was decided that all those who wished to take part in the expected sport, should proceed, and wait their passing this spot, in the hope that some would settle on the branches of the trees. Accordingly, after crossing the river by a rude bridge, which was very nearly half a quarter of a mile in length, we reached the intended spot after wading up to our knees in a swamp or turbary, and getting miserably bemauled by the briars and cane vines. We had not to wait long; the birds, wearied by a long flight, were evidently attracted by the favourable resting-place, and in less than a quarter of an hour, the air was darkened with the hosts hovering over our heads; the sound of their wings defies description, those of my readers who remember the peculiar noise made by a single pigeon in its flight, may form a faint idea by multiplying the sound a million times. It in fact filled the air, and produced a startling effect. Thousands of the birds alighted on the trees, the branches of which snapped and crackled fearfully under the superincumbent load; those of our party who were armed, continued to fire and load as fast as they possibly could. They brought hundreds to the ground, but still, through weariness, perhaps, the rest kept their station on the branches, and did not appear to heed the attack much--shifting their position or only flying off for a moment and then again alighting. By this time many of the settlers from the surrounding districts had arrived to share in the quarry. Thousands of birds were brought to the ground; in fact, every discharge of the guns and rifles brought down showers to our feet; and the noise seemed to resemble our being engaged in action with a foe; without, however, the dire effects of such a rencontre to ourselves. After bagging our game, of which we secured nearly two hundred brace, we returned to the boat, leaving the rest of the sport to those who chose to continue it. We had enough, and, for the remainder of the passage, were completely surfeited with pigeon fare, administered by the boat's cook in all sorts of outlandish forms. In our progress onward through the state, we saw many carcases of these birds outside the villages, such numbers having been destroyed, that the inhabitants could not consume them, and they were accordingly thrown out as refuse. These birds were in good condition, and were excellent eating.

As the packet was likely to be detained for some hours at Zoar, a settlement about two miles beyond Bolivar, owing to a dispute between the captain and some officers connected with the canal, I availed myself of the opportunity, on the invitation of a very gentlemanly fellow-passenger from Connecticut, to visit a farm a few miles in the interior, where resided a celebrated character, named Adam Poe, surnamed by the inhabitants, the "Indian-killer," who had acquired the summit of a backwoods-man's fame, by some forty years ago shooting "Black-foot," a formidable Indian marauder, who, for a long period, spread consternation and alarm among the early settlers. As this exploit (whether justified by the circumstances and times or not, I cannot pretend to say) was one that restored security among the settlers, and dispersed a body of Indians, who destroyed every white inhabitant they encountered, and laid waste their farms, it is no wonder that Adam Poe was regarded as a great man. On arriving at the farm-house, which was one of the better description in that region, we were kindly welcomed by the son of the hero I have mentioned, who bore the father's patronymic, and after the usual hospitality, were ushered into an adjoining apartment, and introduced to the object of our visit. He was sitting in an armchair by the side of his wife, who, like himself, was far advanced in years, their united ages numbering 173. The old man, who was so feeble as to be unable to rise when we entered, saluted us with the usual "Glad to see you, strangers," his spouse at the same time advancing towards us to shake hands. He was evidently used to such intrusions; for, after inquiry where we came from and whither bound, he began, in a tremulous voice, which, from his extreme age, was scarcely intelligible, to narrate his early adventures. It was absolutely shocking, as he became more animated by the subject, to hear the coolness with which the veteran related some of his bloody combats; so much so, indeed, that I and my companion at once cut short his narration, being horrified at the turpitude of the aged sinner, who, although gasping for breath, and evidently on the verge of the unseen world, talked of his deeds of violence with an ardour that befitted a better cause.

The old man dwelt at great length on his hair-breadth escapes and deeds of prowess; but the destruction of the implacable "Black-foot," was the absorbing subject. This chief, it appeared, had, with a small party, been hovering round Poe's farm for several nights, and the inmates were in great terror of a midnight attack; the principal aim of the chief, being, it is supposed to despatch a man, whose activity had rendered him particularly obnoxious to his tribe, and whose bravery was acknowledged by the settlers far and near.

After several nights passed in anxiety, every little circumstance, any unusual noise, the baying of a dog, a disturbance in the hog-pens, exciting the greatest apprehension, Poe determined on stealthily watching the enemy under covert of a hillock or embankment on the farm. He accordingly sallied out with his Indian rifle, in the haze of the evening, taking with him a supply of ***aqua vitae,*** as he facetiously said, to keep up his "dander." After watching a considerable time, every now and then applying his ear to the ground to listen for approaching footsteps (a plan invariably followed by Indians themselves), he ascertained that an Indian was in the vicinity; again intently listening, he soon satisfied himself that the alarm he had experienced was occasioned by one individual only. Instantly on the ***qui-vive,*** he first cocked his rifle, and, just as he descried the Indian's head above the embankment he pulled with unerring aim the fatal trigger, when with an agonizing howl, the Indian toppled backwards down the embankment, and all was silent. Poe now sprang forward, and with his knife severed the "war scalp" from the head of the savage, and after securing his knife and rifle, returned to his home in high glee to announce the horrid achievement. It was, however, deemed unsafe to venture out again that night, for fear of other Indians of Black-foot's band, who it was well known were in the neighbourhood.

In the morning Poe sallied out to the place of reconnoitre with some of the inmates of the farm. Here they found, stretched on the ground, weltering in gore, the vanquished warrior, who was now, for the first time, from a plume he wore, and some other peculiarity in his equipments, identified as the veritable "Sachem," who had for months kept that settlement in a state of alarm. Poe was soon complimented by the settlers around, and from that day forward became a celebrated character.

I was subsequently told on board the canal packet, that the Indian referred to, was not the notorious chief of that name, but a second-rate warrior, who, having headed a band of marauders, ***med the soubriquet. How far this may be the fact, I cannot determine. I, however, frequently heard Poe's name mentioned as a brave defender of the hearths and homes of the early settlers in the remote districts of Ohio.

I could perceive that his son's wife (a matronly dame of about sixty), was adverse to such interviews, as, to use her expression, "they brought the old man back to this world again, when he should be pondering on the next," and that she was grieved at the recital of them; indeed, she several times checked his expressions, when they bordered, as they not unfrequently did, on impiety. She acted rightly, for there was evidently much more of the soldier than the Christian about the old man, and before we left I expressed a hope that such visits would be discouraged, a suggestion that was received in a kindly spirit.

After inspecting the farm, which was well stocked, and appeared to be cultivated in the most approved modern style, and was well fenced with the usual rails, we started on our return to Zoar, where the packet had halted. On our way thither, we passed through a hamlet of primitive appearance, consisting of some half-dozen houses built of logs, at one end of which was a rudely-constructed meeting-house, belonging to the sect of Whitfieldite Methodists. The congregation was assembled, and the horses and vehicles belonging to those who resided at a distance, were tethered and my companion passed, the occupants were chanting a hymn previous to the discourse, which it appeared was a valedictory one, the minister being about to leave this for a more extensive field of pastoral labour. Having time to spare, and such an assembly on a week-day attracting our attention, from its rarity, we stepped in, and remained during the whole of the service, arriving at Zoar a few minutes before the boat started.

As we passed through a densely-wooded district between Bolivar and Chillicothe, I observed that for many miles the trees were denuded of every green leaf, from the devastating effects of millions of locusts, which periodically visit the west-

ern states of the Union, to the dismay of the settlers. The trees in many places were
at the time covered with these destructive insects. I went on shore and procured
several, with the intention of preserving them. They were beautiful creatures, about
ten times the size of an ordinary field grasshopper, and, except that their hind legs
were longer in proportion to their size, the exact shape of that harmless little insect.
Their colours are brilliant green, slate, and flamingo red, beautifully lined and var-
iegated. The humming noise produced by these insects is very disagreeable, and fills
the surrounding air with murmurs, while the wilderness look of the scene of their
depredations has a depressing effect on the mind of the traveller. Their visits are
much dreaded, as they are followed by the total destruction of foliage in the district,
and in many instances, the young saplings die in consequence of their attacks.

After a pleasant passage of four or five days, the packet arrived at the river
junction; and taking passage at once in a steamer which was waiting its arrival in
the Ohio river, I was soon rapidly on my way to that fairy city of the west, Cincinnati. This is the largest city in the state of Ohio, and is the capital of Hamilton
county. Fort Washington, a defence of some renown during the war, is two miles
above, and opposite to the mouth of the Licking river. The broad bosom of the Ohio
was here covered with steam-boats, employed in the Virginia, Missouri, and New
Orleans trade. The wharves are commodious, and a broad inclined plane, from the
city to the water's edge, gives the former a fine appearance, as it rests majestically
in the background.

As I was anxious to proceed to the State of Missouri, with as little delay as
possible, I at once engaged a passage to St. Louis, and the following morning was
steaming in the direction of the falls of St. Anthony. The passengers in this boat
employed themselves nearly the whole of the route at games of cards, *faro* being
the favourite. This predilection for gambling, which is generally carried to great
extremes on board southern boats, was not, however, confined to the cabin, for I
noticed the crew, at every spare interval, sitting about on deck, with packs of cards,
completely absorbed in the game. The negro hands were particularly addicted to
this vice, and a gentleman who was proceeding in the boat informed me that but a
trifle of the earnings of boat-hands in general was spared from their devotedness to
this ruinous practice. The effect of association with, and the example set by, white
men given to gambling, will account, perhaps, for the habit. This moral pestilence

is in vain prohibited by the state, and is pursued by all classes in the south with frenzied avidity.

After twice running on shore, and meeting with sundry other stoppages and minor mishaps, through the mismanagement of the two engineers, we reached the city of St. Louis, to the gratification of myself and fellow-passengers. This is a place of considerable extent, although awkwardly built, and for the most part irregularly laid out. It is a considerable fur depot of the Hudson Bay Company; and there is a recruiting station, from whence start expeditions of trappers to the Rocky Mountains. I saw a large party of these adventurers, who were about to start on an expedition to these remote confines. It consisted entirely of young Frenchmen and Hollanders, who are preferred for the service by the company. They were of slight make, and little calculated, from their appearance, to encounter the hardships of such a life; but I was told they soon become hardened, and return strong, athletic men. The employment is, however, beset with danger, from the hostile dispositions of the various tribes of Indians in the western wilds, who view their intrusion with vindictive feelings, and seize every opportunity of attacking and annihilating small parties, notwithstanding their professions of friendship. Not long after my arrival, a party of trappers arrived from the Upper Missouri in two boats, which were loaded with buffalo and other furs. The stalwart look of these hardy mountaineers proved the hardening effect of their mode of life. They were brawny fellows of a ruddy brown complexion, of the true Indian hue, and habited in skins. These men, I ascertained, had been in the mountains for four or five years, during which time they had subsisted entirely on Buffalo and other meat, bread not being used or cared for. Their healthy look under such circumstances completely shook my faith in the Brahminical vegetarian theory, and goes far, I think, to prove that man was intended by his Maker to be a carnivorous animal.

Just before the steamer approached the city, a circumstance occurred on board that filled me and my fellow-passengers with horror. We were taking breakfast in the cabin, congratulating each other on the near termination of our tedious passage, when a sudden shriek, followed by shouts from the deck-hands of the vessel, disturbed our meal. Hastening in great perturbation to the deck, we soon discovered the cause of the disturbance. One of the white waiters was lying on the deck, with a frightful gash in his side, from which the blood was fast oozing. Our first care was to attend to the sufferer, and a surgeon being fortunately amongst the passengers, the hemorrhage was soon abated, but the wound was pronounced to be of a fatal character. The poor fellow, who was a lad of about eighteen years of age, moaned piteously. Every attention that skill and kindness could suggest was paid to him. He was immediately carried to a state-room in the cabin, where he remained in great agony until the vessel was moored alongside the levee, when he was carefully removed on a litter to a hospital on shore. The perpetrator of the savage act proved to be a negro, filling the office of assistant cook. The passengers were very clamorous, and would, without doubt, have hanged the culprit immediately, had it not been for the interference of the captain, who, after a curt examination, had him pinioned and taken below. From the version given of the affair by the negroes who witnessed it (but which was contradicted by two white men who were on the spot), I was inclined to think the crime was committed under feelings of great provocation, the negro, as is commonly the case on board steam-boats, having been for a long time browbeaten by the victim of the sad catastrophe, and subjected to very insolent and overbearing treatment at his hands. The culprit, who was a very sullen, stolid-looking, full-bred negro, refused to answer the questions put to him on the subject, and certainly manifested a careless indifference to consequences that was not in his favour; his fierce scowl denoting great ferocity, in all probability induced by long ill-treatment. As soon as convenience allowed, some officers from the shore came on board and secured the prisoner, who was conveyed by them to the city gaol, to await the investigation of the outrage by the civic authorities and the result of the injury committed. The victim of revenge died a few days after the occurrence in excruciating agony. It will scarcely be believed that the perpetrator of the deed, after a short confinement, was spirited away up the country, no doubt at the connivance of the authorities, and sold!

Thus, justice is often defeated, from pecuniary considerations in the Slave States of America, where, if a slave commits even the heinous crime of murder, the ordinary course of the law is interfered with to save the owner from loss. This of itself is sufficient to stamp for ever as infamous the social cancer of slavery, and brands as ridiculous, the boasted regard for justice, so pragmatically urged in the southern states of the American continent.

A mile or two from St. Louis, on the Carondelet road, are situated spacious infantry barracks, named after Jefferson, one of the former presidents of the Union, where troops are stationed in readiness to act against the various tribes of Indians in the Upper Missouri country, who sometimes show a disposition to be hostile. A reserve of troops is more particularly needful for the protection of the inhabitants; for, either from mismanagement or an aggressive spirit, the Government is continually embroiled with the aboriginal tribes in harassing and expensive warfare. This state of things acts as a perpetual blister, and has engendered a rancorous enmity between the Indians and their white neighbours, to the great detriment of peaceful agricultural pursuits by the latter, and the periodical perplexity of the Chancellor of the American Exchequer; whereas, a conciliating policy would not only keep the tribes in close friendship, but secure their services as valuable allies in case of emergency--a point that may possibly suggest itself eventually to the executive, if the rampant spirit of aggrandisement now abroad continues to govern the public mind in America.

Soon after landing, I was accosted by a middle-aged gentlemanly man, on the subject of the outrage on board the boat, and as he appeared to have less of that swaggering air about him than most men in the south possess, I entered freely into conversation with him, and in a very short time our interchange of sentiments created a mutual partiality, that led to his inviting me to pass the following evening at his house, a result I rather wished for, as he manifested a disposition to inform me fully on several questions I put to him relative to the state I was now in and my future movements; moreover, he seemed somewhat attached to the English, or rather was not strong in his prejudices against them.

I accordingly repaired to his residence at the time appointed. This was situated in one of the lateral streets of the city leading to the outskirts, and, although not large, was furnished with great taste and elegance. His lady, who was, I think, from Illinois, made herself very agreeable, her kind attentions tending to confirm the impression I already entertained of her countrywomen; they had no children, and the husband was engaged in some way with the Fur Company established in St. Louis. I was entertained with great hospitality; my kind host materially assisting me by information, &c. in my intention to pursue my route south.

He was the son of a New Englander, or native of one of the eastern states; his father having fought at Bunker's Hill, and otherwise taken an active part in the struggle for independence, between the years 1776 and 1785. This made it the more extraordinary that he should treat an Englishman with the courtesy he showed to me, especially as under such circumstances a bias is in general handed down from father to son, which operates prejudicially to my countrymen.

After putting a variety of questions, as to the "old country" as he termed Great Britain, on which I readily satisfied his curiosity, he entered into a detail of some of the stirring events relating to the period of his father's career in arms against the British; some of these were of a thrilling character, and strongly depicted the miseries of war, presenting a lamentable picture of the debasing influence of sanguinary struggles on the human mind. The barbarous mode of harassing the British troops, by picking off stragglers, which the lower orders of Americans pursued, in most instances for the sake of the wretched clothing and accoutrements of the victims, the former being dyed of a dark colour, and sold for a dollar per set (as he called the military suit), to the American citizen-soldiers, fairly made my blood creep; one instance in particular filled me with horror, for it was a cold-blooded murder of the deepest dye I must, however, do the narrator the justice to say that he viewed the atrocity in the same light as I did.

The occurrence I am about to relate, took place somewhere on the banks of the Hudson, below West Point, where a force of British troops were encamped or pursuing their operations under the protection of some vessels of war lying in the stream, he mentioned the exact spot where it occurred, but I have forgotten it. It appeared that this force was harassed and beset by parties of citizens, who, by pursuing a guerilla system of warfare, surprising small parties, and firing entirely in ambush, made great havoc amongst the rank and file of the invaders, almost every straggler falling a victim. One evening, during this state of things, two of the citizens, whilst prowling in a coppice, within a few miles of the camp, on the look-out, came suddenly upon an infantry soldier, who was off his guard at the moment, and whose firelock was resting against a tree; the foremost of the Americans darted forward and seized the weapon, while the second captured the wretched soldier. Under ordinary circumstances, and in more honourable hands, the man would have been conveyed as a prisoner of war to the American camp, but plunder being their object, this would not answer the purpose of the miscreants, the most resolute of whom ordered the captive (who was a lad of seventeen or eighteen), to take off his jacket. Knowing this was a preliminary step to his being shot, he fell on his knees and implored mercy. His captors were, however, inexorable, and he began to cry bitterly, and besought them to spare his life; these manifestations had, however, no effect on his deadly foes, who now threatened to fell him with the butt end of a fusee if he did not comply: this had the effect, and the poor captive reluctantly pulled off the jacket and threw it on the ground; this was immediately picked up by one of the party, to avoid its being stained with the life-blood of the victim. Withdrawing now a few paces, one of the Americans took a deliberate aim; the young soldier instantly turned to run, but as he wheeled round for the purpose (for his enemies were facing him), a ball entered his left side, just under the armpit, and springing frantically several feet into the air, he fell dead to the ground. He was then stripped, and left on the spot.

This horrid relation I should have thought, for the credit of his country, an American would have kept secret; but as I before observed, he was by no means disposed to take the part of these so-called patriots, although he stated that many atrocities were committed by the British, some of which he related, and which were, he said, never recorded; these, I fear, if exposed, would not much redound to their credit with the present generation.

At first I could not understand why the soldier was ordered before being shot to pull his jacket off; this he explained by saying, that a rent in the garment made by the ball of a fusee, would have lessened its value; and further, that the American soldiers were averse, from superstitious fear at the time, to wearing any article of dress in which an enemy had yielded his breath; notwithstanding which repugnance, the American soldiers not long after dismissed the objection, from the extreme scantiness of the clothing afforded them.

On my intimating the abhorrence I felt at the relation, my entertainer informed me that it was impossible at the time to prevent such occurrences, the annihilation of the invaders was the *primum mobile* of all Americans, and many citizens harassed the enemy on their own account, the principle being the same on which European vessels bearing letters of marque, are suffered to waylay and seize, for the purpose of private gain, the merchant vessels belonging to the country with which they are at war. Such atrocities, as he remarked, however horrifying in times of peace, are of every-day occurrence between contending armies.

Amongst those I had occasion to call on at St. Louis, was a Major ----. He had formerly been engaged in Indian warfare, and, having received a wound from a rifle-ball, that incapacitated him for active military duty, he was living as a retired citizen--his wife's jointure, and an allowance from Government, allowing him to keep up a tolerably good establishment. He was the owner of several slaves, and, amongst the rest, a young woman who was employed as nursemaid in the family. The first time I called at his residence, I thought him a man of superior manners and education, and was much pleased with the visit, which was concluded with a promise to renew it on a future day. When, however, I repeated my visit soon after, I found him alone in his study, and his constrained manner soon led me to perceive that something unusual perturbed his mind. The cause was soon after explained, for, the negress, before mentioned, coming into the room on some trifling errand, to my surprise accosted him rather freely. Her master suddenly broke out in a paroxysm of rage, swore at her awfully, and accused her in a ruffianly way of being insolent to her mistress. Then, violently ringing a bell which stood on the table, he summoned a negro lad into the room, and at once despatched him to a neighbour's house to borrow a new raw-hide whip, threatening all the while to flay her alive. In vain the terrified creature pleaded innocence; he would take no excuse, and, although I begged earnestly for him to pass over the offence, and the poor slave fell on her knees in the greatest terror, he vowed vengeance with dreadful imprecations. At last the whip came, and, disregarding alike the presence of a stranger, and the entreaties of a woman, he began the flagellation with murderous earnest. My interference only added to his ungovernable rage. The raw-hide was new, and the major being a strong, muscular man, every stroke told. The blood soon flowed from the back, neck, and breasts, of the poor victim, whose cries, as she writhed under the savage infliction, entered my soul. They, however, made no impression on her brutal tormentor, who kept vociferating with all his energy to keep her quiet. It was with some difficulty I stood by and witnessed the assault, but I well know my life would be in jeopardy if I attempted to interfere. I, however, screwed up my courage to stay, in the hope that some sense of shame might induce the fellow to hold his hand. This was, however, a delusive hope, for he continued to lay on the whip until he was exhausted.

The girl was now on the floor of the room, moaning piteously, and a stream of blood was flowing from her lacerated person, which soaked the matting that covered the floor. Her dress was hanging in tatters, and the blood trickling down her cheeks had a horrifying effect. As soon as the ruffian was tired, he bid the woman get down stairs and wash herself. The miserable creature arose with difficulty, and picking up her apron and turban, which were in different parts of the room, she hobbled out crying bitterly. As soon as she was gone, the major pointed to the blood, and said, "If we did not see that sometimes, there would be no living with the brutes;" to which I replied in terms he could not misunderstand, and at once left the house, determined never again to enter it--a resolution I religiously kept. I afterwards heard that this miserable creature was pregnant at the time, a circumstance that would have induced at least some regard to leniency in any man not utterly debased.

Those who are acquainted with southern scenes will see nothing extraordinary in this recital, for they are every-day occurrences, and scarcely elicit a remark, unless the perpetrator should happen to be a slave-holding Wesleyan or Whitfieldite, when, perhaps, he would be called to some account--his own version of the affair being of course admitted *in limine*. Many of the slave-holders are an incorrigibly degraded set of men. It is by no means uncommon for them to inflict chastisement on negresses with whom they are in habitual illicit intercourse, and I was credibly informed that this cruelty was often resorted to, to disabuse the mind of a deceived and injured wife who suspects unfair treatment. This attested fact, disgraceful as it is, can scarcely be wondered at in men who mercilessly subject defenceless women to the lash without a spark of human feeling, or compunction of conscience. It is little to the credit of United States senators that they have not at least made laws to protect women from the barbarous usage of flogging. One would imagine that men, who, perhaps, above all others in the world, pay homage to the sex, would have established a distinction in this respect; but I apprehend the truth to be, that they are so far influenced by their wives, who are notoriously jealous of their sable rivals, that they have succumbed to their sentiments and dictation.

There are many Dutch in St. Louis, and along the levee you perceive boarding-houses and groceries kept for their accommodation. These men are generally great drinkers, and think as little of quaffing at a few draughts half-a-pint of whiskey, as an Englishman would the same quantity of malt liquor. They consume, also, vast quantities of claret. I have frequently seen a couple of these men at a cafe, drink five or bottles without betraying any ill effects. It must, however, be remembered that claret is not so potent as the heavier wines.

A few days after my arrival, while standing in the vestibule of my hotel, my attention was drawn to a loud altercation going on at the bar, and as it was evident, from the manner of the parties, that some public question was being discussed, I listened, and ascertained that an obnoxious citizen had been seized for perpetrating a petty act of revenge on a neighbour by damaging his horse, and was that day to be publicly tarred, feathered, and escorted out of the city, as they said, bag and baggage. Having ascertained the spot selected for the scene, I determined to witness it. Accordingly, at noon, the appointed hour, I repaired to an open spot of building-land on the Carondelet side of the city. Here I found assembled a motley assemblage of citizens, negroes, steamboat-hands, and the general riff-raff of the place. Although the crowd was not so great, the meeting strongly reminded me of those scenes of infamy and disgrace in England--public executions; the conduct of the assembled throng on this occasion being the more decorous of the two. Precisely at twelve, the mob made a rush towards one corner of the open space, from which direction I saw the culprit advancing, in charge of thirty or forty well-dressed people (the committee appointed for the occasion being among the number). He was a stout man, and described to me as a great bully; but now he looked completely crest-fallen. As the party came on, he was hissed by the mob, who, however, kept at a good distance from his guard. A man, with a large tin can of smoking pitch, a brush of the kind used in applying the same, and a pillow of feathers under his arm, followed immediately behind the prisoner, vociferating loudly. Arrived at the spot, the poor wretch was placed on a stool, and a citizen, who had taken a very prominent part in front of the procession, and who, I was told, was the chief cause of this outrage, stepped in front of him, and pulling out a sheet of paper, read a lecture on the enormity of his crime, which wound up with the sentence about to be enforced. When this was finished, the man who carried the tar-vessel stepped up, and began, with a scissors, to cut off the culprit's hair, which he did most effectually, flinging portions amongst the crowd, who scrambled after them. As soon as this was finished, and the man was stripped to the waist, the brush was dipped into the pitch, and the upper part of his person lathered therewith. Not a word escaped him, but the individual who had taken so prominent a part in the punishment, kept giving directions to the operator to put it on thick. Even his eyes and ears were not spared. As soon as this part of the operation was complete, the bag of feathers was ripped open by a by-stander, and the contents stuck thickly on the parts besmeared with tar, amidst the deafening cheers of the spectators, who were by this time in such frantic excitement that I began to fear a tragedy would ensue, especially as many of them shouted, "Now hang the varmint! hang him!" This proposal was eagerly seconded by the mob. This was, however, resolutely overruled by his keepers. The appearance presented by the victim, in this peculiarly American dress, was ludicrous in the extreme, and *looked* very comfortable. As soon as this part of the exhibition was finished, a man, with a small drum, followed by the mob, with yells and execrations drove the culprit before them at a run. The poor wretch ran like a deer from his pursuers, who followed at his heels, shouting frantically, until he reached the brink of the river, where a boat was waiting to take him off. He dashed into it, and was at once rowed into the middle of the stream, out of reach of his tormentors, who, I quite believe, would have administered more severe lynch-law if they could have got hold of him, for their passions were wrought up to the highest pitch of excitement. One feature in the scene I could not help remarking--the negroes all appeared in high glee, and many of them actually danced with joy. I did not wonder at this, for the negroes always seemed to exult if a white man was in disgrace; which, after all, is no more than might be expected from a class of men tyrannized over as the coloured people are there, and is one of the results of the oppressive system that exacts everything that human labour can furnish, without remuneration, and without (in by far the greater number of instances) any approach to sympathy or grateful feeling. This alone, without taking into consideration the outrages inflicted on the race by their cruel oppressors, supplies a sufficient cause for such a tendency, if every other were wanting.

Passing through the principal street the day before I left St Louis, an assembly of men, chiefly overseers and negro dealers, who stood at the entrance of a large store, attracted my attention. Large placards, with a description of various lots of negroes to be submitted to public competition, soon told me I should now be able to gratify my curiosity by witnessing a Missouri slave-vendue. A man with a bell, which he rang most energetically at the door, shortly after summoned the company, the auction being about to commence. On a table inside, a negress, of a little over middle age, was standing, vacantly gazing with grief-worn countenance on the crowd that now thronged to the table. On the floor stood two children, of about the ages of ten and thirteen respectively. The auctioneer, with the customary volubility of such men in America, began by stating, that the lots now to be offered were the remnants of a preceding sale, which he gratuitously observed had been a most satisfactory one, and after dilating with some energy on the good qualities of the woman before us, whose face brightened up a little on hearing such a flattering account of her good qualities, he earnestly requested a bidding. The poor creature was evidently in ill-health. After the most revolting questions had been put to her, and her person examined by the competitors with disgraceful familiarity, she was pronounced all but worthless, "used up," as one of the company observed, and was, after much demur on the part of the auctioneer, knocked down for two hundred dollars; this sum being, as he remarked, but the moiety of what she ought to have realized. She was then roughly told to get off the table, and take her stand near it, at a place pointed out by her purchaser, who was a rollicking-looking, big-whiskered fellow, with an immense Leghorn hat, the brim of which was lined with black, and having a broad black ribbon round the crown. As the poor woman got down, she cast a furtive glance at her children, who, although the auctioneer certainly tried to prevent it, were sold to two individuals, neither of whom was the purchaser of the parent. The poor woman looked about in great despair while the bidding was going on. It was in vain I sought one sympathizing look in that company; but how could it be expected, when it consisted of men long inured to such heartless scenes--men whose hearts were case-hardened by the impious traffic they were now engaged in. I was, however, pleased to hear afterwards that the purchasers all resided in St. Louis, and that the woman would often see her children--poor amends it is true for a cruel separation, but more satisfactory than such cases generally are.

CHAPTER IV.

"Where Will-o'-the-wisps and glow-worms shine,
In bulrush and in brake;
Where waving mosses shroud the pine,
And the cedar grows, and the poisonous vine
Is spotted like the snake."--LONGFELLOW.

From St. Louis, on the Missouri river, I took passage to New Orleans, in one of those magnificent steamers that crowd the inland waters of the American continent, and which, sumptuously furnished as they are, have not inaptly been termed "floating palaces." We had a prosperous passage as far as the junction of the Ohio with the Mississippi, where the boat struck the branches of a large tree, that had been washed into the bed of the stream, and was there stuck fast, root downwards. This formidable chevaux-de-frise (or snag, as it was termed by the captain) fortunately did not do much damage to the vessel, although at first an alarm was raised that she was sinking, and much confusion ensued. This apprehension was, however, soon dissipated by the report of the carpenter, whose account of the damage was so far favourable, that after extrication by backing the vessel, and a few temporary repairs, she was again got under headway.

The pellucid waters of the Ohio, as they enter the turbid rushing current of the Mississippi, which is swollen by the Illinois and other tributaries, has a remarkable effect, the clear current of the former river refusing, for a considerable distance, to mingle with the murky stream of the latter, and forming a visible blue channel in its centre--a phenomenon I thought allegorical of the slave-stained condition of the one state, and the free soil of the other, for while Ohio is free from the curse of slavery, the banks of the Mississippi have for centuries been deep dyed in the life's blood of the oppressed African.

Our vessel was borne on the rushing waters with great impetuosity, the maddening current of the Mississippi seeming to carry everything before it. As we proceeded we constantly saw trees topple over into the river, the banks of which are continually widening, and which in many parts has the appearance of a lake after a storm, impregnated with debris. The trees, thus washed into the bed of the river, sink root downwards and make the navigation perilous, as I have before described. We met numerous steamers coming up the stream, one of them having a freight of Indians from Florida, removing to the western frontier, under the surveillance of U.S. soldiery and government agents. The compulsory removal of Indians, from one remote state to another, whenever new territory is needed, forms a disgraceful feature in internal American policy. Transported to new hunting grounds, the poor Indians are brought into contact with other tribes, when feuds arise from feelings of jealousy, and the new-comers are often annihilated in a few years. Many tribes have thus become totally extinct, and the remainder are rapidly becoming so. As the steamer passed us with her freight of red men they set up a loud yell, which reverberated through the forests on the river-shores. It sounded to me very much like defiance, and probably was, for they execrate the white men as hereditary enemies, and feel deeply the wrongs inflicted on their people.

All the steamers we met were more or less crowded with passengers, the visages of many of whom bore traces of fever and ague, and who were, doubtless, removing to a healthier climate. This insidious disease often terminates fatally in the cities and districts skirting the swamps of Louisiana, and, to avoid its baneful effects, the more affluent people migrate south-west or north when the sickly season sets in. The yellow fever is also very fatal in such situations, and annually claims numbers of victims.

We had by this time reached that latitude where perpetual summer reigns. The banks of the mighty Mississippi, which has for ages rolled on in increasing grandeur, present to the eye a wilderness of sombre scenery, indescribably wild and romantic. The bays, formed by the current, are choked with palmetto and other trees, and teem with alligators, water-snakes, and freshwater turtle, the former basking in the sun in conscious security. Overhead, pelicans, paroquets, and numberless other

"Strange bright birds on their starry wings,   Bear the rich hues of all glorious things;"

while the gorgeous magnolia, in luxuriant bloom, and a thousand other ever-greens, on shore, vie with voluptuous aquatic flowers to bewilder and delight the astonished traveller, accustomed hitherto only to the more unassuming productions of the sober north. Everything here was new, strange, and solemn. The gigantic trees, encircled by enormous vines, and heavily shrouded in grey funereal moss, mournfully waving in the breeze--the doleful night-cry of the death-bird and the whip-poor-will--the distant bugle of the advancing boats--the moan of the turbid current beneath--the silent and queenly moon above, appearing nearer, larger, and brighter than in our cooler latitudes--the sultry atmosphere--and most of all, per-haps, the sense of the near vicinity of death in this infected region--oppressed my spirit with an ominous feeling of solemnity and awe.

As we passed the plantations which here and there varied the scene, gangs of negroes could be seen at labour--their sturdy overseers, of ruffianly mien, prowl-ing sulkily about, watching every motion of the bondsmen, whip in hand; which weapon they applied with the most wanton freedom, as if the poor sufferers were as destitute of physical sensation, as they themselves were of moral or humane feeling. Armed with a huge bowie-knife and pistols, these embruted creatures were very cut-throats in appearance; and it is well known there, that their conduct in general towards those they lord over, justifies the appellation I have given them.

The steamer halted at intervals to take in wood, which is invariably used, in-stead of coal as in England. This is piled in parrallelograms on the banks--the logs being split longitudinally. This forms a source of good profit, and is, in many in-stances, the chief maintenance of the squalid settlers of these plague-stricken and unwholesome places. After the measurement of the pile by the mate or captain, the deck-passengers and boat-hands stow it away in the vicinity of the furnaces--it be-ing part of the terms of passage, that the lower order of passengers shall assist in the operation. This is much disliked by the latter, and many of the Germans of this class on board, endeavoured to escape the laborious duty by hiding amongst the packages on deck. A general search was, however, instituted by the officers of the vessel, just before it stopped at a wooding-station--and the skulkers were brought out, amidst the clamorous jeers of their fellows. The class of passengers I have just referred to, consisted chiefly of Germans and Irish, who, although there is no professed dis-tinction, bargain for a deck-passage, the charge being better suited to their means.

Amongst the objects that arrested my attention, as our vessel floated majestically down the turbid current, were gibbets standing on the banks, depending from several of which were short chains, doubtless required occasionally in carrying out this kind of discipline. As the horrifying objects occurred at intervals of a few miles, I at first imagined they were cranes used to lower bales of cotton into the holds of vessels, and addressing a passenger whose physiognomy prepossessed me in his favour, and who had several times shown a disposition to impart the knowledge he possessed concerning the objects around, he soon convinced me of my mistake, adding, that such engines were as necessary to the proper discipline of the negroes in that latitude as the overseer himself. He then proceeded to detail several instances of fugitive negroes being dragged in capture to the foot of the gallows, where, with halter-encircled necks, they were made not only to acknowledge the error committed and expose accessories, but "pumped dry," as he facetiously termed it, as to the intended flight of other negroes on the estate. Sometimes, he said, it was necessary to suspend the culprit for a moment or so, to intimidate, but this was only in cases where the victim (he used the word rascal) was inclined to be sullen, and refused readily to give the required information. I inquired whether it ever occurred that actual execution took place; to this my new acquaintance replied, "Wall, yes, where the nigger had dar'd to strike a white man;" but that it was usual to go to a magistrate first, in such cases. The appearance of these gibbets, after the information I had received respecting them from my slave-holding acquaintance, made my flesh creep as we steamed onwards, the more so as, in many of the grounds skirting the river, where these sombre murky-looking objects presented themselves to the gaze of the traveller, gangs of negroes were at work, looking up complacently for a moment as the vessel glided by. I was subsequently told by a gentleman who had been long resident in the state of Louisiana, that no punishment so effectually strikes with terror the negro mind, as that of hanging, the very threat being sufficient to subdue (in general) the most hardened offenders. This I do not wonder at, for perhaps there are few field-hands living in the south but have, at some time or other, witnessed the barbarities used at a negro execution, sudden death by pistol or bowie knife being far preferable to the brutal sneers and indignities heaped upon the victim by the cowardly assassins who superintend such operations.

The monotony of the scenes which had for a thousand miles rendered the passage irksome, began to break as we approached Natchez. This place takes its name from the Natch-i-toches, or Red River, which falls into the Mississippi, the abbreviation being a corruption of the original Indian name, which is as above stated. The town stands on a declivity or bluff, and is of considerable extent. I did not visit it, although the boat halted for a considerable time, to land letter-bags and passengers. I was informed by a fellow-passenger of gentlemanly bearing, who resided in the vicinity, that it was a dissipated place, and gambling the chief occupation of its inhabitants. The locality has been remarkable for landslips, owing to the siliceous nature of the soil; I saw traces of a fearful catastrophe of the kind which had, some time before, buried or destroyed many of the houses and their occupants, the enormous mass having also sunk several steam-boats and other vessels which were moored at the foot of the bluff under the town.

After leaving Natchez, we steamed away with renewed vigour towards that centre of slavery and dissipation, New Orleans, and were in due course moored to the levee, which extends the whole river-length of the city, and is about a mile in extent. The first news I heard, and which alarmed me not a little, was that the yellow fever was at this time raging in the city. New Orleans is just fifty-four miles from the mouth of the Mississippi, and being built at the time of the Orleans Regency, contains many ancient structures. Its inhabitants, even to this day, are to a great extent either French or of Gaelic origin. It lies exceedingly flat, which causes the locality to be unhealthy and ill-suited to European constitutions; the soil is, however, fertile and rich; this is, perhaps, to be accounted for by the constant irrigation it undergoes from the overflowing of the Mississippi, which, like another Nile, periodically submerges the country around its banks. The town is situated on the east side of the river.

The vast quantity of shipping of all classes in the harbour is a very striking feature in this extensive and wealthy city. The bad eminence to which New Orleans has attained is painful to contemplate. Its wealth is purchased by the blood and tears of thousands of slaves, who are daily exposed like cattle in its markets; and this fact operates on the mind of an Englishman to the prejudice of its inhabitants. I was myself filled with disgust towards the whites, as well as pity towards the blacks, on beholding, immediately on our arrival, a gang of forty or fifty negroes, of both sexes, and nearly all ages, working in shackles on the wharf. These, I was informed, were principally captured fugitives; they looked haggard and care-worn, and as they toiled with their barrows with uncovered heads, under a burning sun, they were mercilessly lashed with a heavy slave-whip, by a tall, athletic negro, who acted as overseer, and who, with refined cruelty, dispensed the punishment alike on stout men, slender youths, and thin attenuated females. Our arrival having attracted the notice of the gang, and induced a momentary halt in their work, the unfeeling wretch commenced a furious onslaught with the whip, each crack of which, followed, as it was, by the groans or cries of the sufferer, roused the indignant feelings of the passengers, many of whom were from the free states, and who simultaneously raised a yell of execration which made the welkin resound, and caused the cruel driver to stand aghast. This demonstration drew a remonstrance from the captain, who represented to the passengers the danger of such conduct, and concluded by observing that if it was repeated, it would probably arouse the indignation of the citizens, who were very bigoted. He should be sorry, he added, to be obliged to put the vessel about again, a proceeding that might be necessary for the safety of all on board, unless they were more cautious. Some of the passengers seemed disposed to dispute this argument, but they were overruled by the majority, who, better acquainted with southern usages, prejudices, and barbarities, thought that discretion under the circumstances would be the better part of valour. I afterwards found that the captain's view was a strictly correct one, for so jealous are the citizens of men entertaining hostility to the pro-slavery cause, that spies are often sent on board newly-arrived boats, to ascertain if missionaries are amongst the passengers. These spies, with Jesuitical art, introduce themselves by making apparently casual inquiries on leading topics of those they suspect, and if their end is subserved, basely betray them, or, what is more usual, keep them under strict surveillance, with a view to their being detected in disseminating abolition doctrines amongst the slaves, when they are immediately made amenable to the laws, and are fined or imprisoned.

On landing, I hired a sorry conveyance, driven by a creole and drawn by a mule, and had my luggage taken to a house in the suburbs, where I had been recommended to take up my residence during my stay, which, owing to the presence of the yellow fever, that daily carried off numbers of victims, I had determined, contrary to my original intention, should be short.

The crowds of people on the levee, attracted by the constant arrival of steam-boats, had a motley appearance; many of these were rough-looking fellows, fit for any occupation, most of them being armed with bowie knives, the silver hilts of which could often be seen peering suspiciously from under the waistcoat, in the inner lining of which a case or scabbard of leather is sewn for the reception of the weapon. The vast proportion of blacks in the streets soon struck me. I should think they were five to one of the white population. These, for the most part, wore in wretched plight; many of them begged of the passers-by, which practice I found afterwards to be very general, especially in the suburbs of the city.

Amongst the passengers on our boat, was a person, apparently of the better class, who was met at the levee by two black servants with a carriage. I noticed particularly, that, although the negroes touched their hats, and inquired how he was (by which I concluded he had been absent for some time), he did not deign to answer their inquiries. From their timidity, it was evident that he was an overbearing man, and the imperial haughtiness manifested in giving them his orders, confirmed this impression. This individual was one of those who condemned the demonstration I have noticed, when the boat first approached the levee.

After a day's rest at my boarding-house, I walked through the city, and afterwards visited the calaboose, which in New Orleans is a mart for produce, as well as a place of detention and punishment for slaves. Here those owners who are averse to correcting their slaves in a rigorous manner at home, send them to be flogged. The brutal way in which this is done at the calaboose, strikes terror into the negro mind, and the threat is often sufficient to tame the most incorrigible. Instances, I was told, have often occurred of negroes expiring under the severity of the discipline here; but it was remarked that the pecuniary loss attendant on such casualties made the keepers careful not to exceed the physical endurance of the sufferer, and that they were so well acquainted with negro constitutions that it was a rare exception for death to ensue. The punishment, however, almost always resulted in the victim being invalided and unfitted for exertion for a considerable time.

I believe New Orleans to be as vile a place as any under the sun; a perfect Ghetto or cursed place; in fact, it is the rendezvous of renegades of all nations, and hordes of negro traders and planters are to be seen flocking round the hotels. These are extensive patrons of the gambling-houses; and the faro, ***rouge-et-noir,*** roulette, and other establishments, fitted up with gorgeous saloons, are generally crowded with them. As you pass, you may observe the frequenters of such places in dozens, deeply engaged in play, while the teller of the establishment sits at a table with a huge heap of Spanish doubloons or Mexican mill dollars before him, which he adds to or takes from with the tact of a banker's clerk, as the chances of luck may arise. Violence and Woodshed have been indigenous to this city from time immemorial, and feuds are instantly settled by an appeal to the bowie knife, or ever-ready revolver. Highway robberies are very frequent, and I was told it was more than your life was worth to be out after dark, in certain localities, unless armed and on your guard. The police authorities are, nevertheless, vigilant, and the magistrates severe, so that many desperadoes are brought to justice.

The suburbs of New Orleans lie low, and the swampy soil emits a poisonous miasma. This is, without doubt, the cause of virulent epidemics that visit the city annually with direful effect. Thousands fly to the northern states, to escape the contagion; but there are many who, for want of means, are obliged to risk a continued residence at such periods, and it is amongst those that the yellow fever, the ague, or the flux, plays dreadful havoc. It is the custom for the small store-keepers, as well as the more affluent merchants, to confide their affairs at such seasons to others, and I have frequently seen advertisements in the *New Orleans Picayune*, and other papers, offering a gratuity to persons to undertake the charge in their absence.

The heat, although the summer was not far advanced, was excessive, and the thousands of mosquitoes that filled the air, especially after a fall of rain, when they seemed to burst into life in myriads spontaneously, kept up an increasing annoyance. At night this was ten-fold, for notwithstanding the gauze awnings, or bars, as they are called, which completely enveloped the bedstead, to the floor of the room, they found admittance with pertinacious audacity, and kept up a buzzing and humming about my ears that almost entirely deprived me of rest. This unceasing nuisance in the hot season, makes it difficult to keep one's equanimity of temper, and has, probably, much to do with that extreme irascibility shown by the southern inhabitants of the American continent.

The appearance and situation of hundreds of quadroon females in this city, soon attracted my attention, and deserve notice. I saw numbers of them not only at the bazaars or shops making purchases, but riding in splendid carriages through the streets. So prodigal are these poor deluded creatures of their money, that, although slaves and liable to immediate sale at the caprice of their keepers, they have often been known to spend in one afternoon 200 dollars in a shopping excursion. Endowed with natural talents, they are readily instructed in every accomplishment, requisite to constitute them charming companions. Often as a carriage dashes by, the pedestrian is able to catch a glimpse of some jewelled and turbaned sultana, of dazzling beauty, attended by her maid, who does not always possess a sinecure, for the mistress is often haughty, proud, and petulant, very hard to please, and exacts great deference from her inferiors. Many of them live in regal splendour, and everything that wealth and pampered luxury can bestow is theirs, as long as their personal charms remain; but when their beauty has ceased to gratify the passions of their masters, they are, in most instances, cast off, and frequently die in a condition which presents the greatest possible contrast to their former gay but not happy life.

"Oh that they had earlier died,
Sleeping calmly side by side,
Where the tyrant's power is o'er,
And the fetter galls no more."

Many of such poor outcasts are to be found scattered all over the slave states, some employed as field hands, but in general they are selected as domestics, their former habits of luxury and ease rendering their constitutions too delicate for the exposure of ordinary field labour. It is not, however, as the reader will have observed, commiseration that saves them from that degradation. As soon as beauty begins to fade, which in southern climes it does prematurely, the unfeeling owners of these unfortunates succeed in ridding themselves of what is now considered a burden, by disposing of the individual to some heartless trader. This is done unknown to the victim, and the news, when it reaches her, drives her almost frantic; she at once seeks her perfidious paramour, and finds to her dismay, that he has been gone some days on a tour to the provinces, and is, perhaps, a thousand miles off. Tears and protestations avail her nothing, the trader is inexorable, she belongs to him by law, and go she must; at length, having vainly expended her entreaties, she becomes calm, and submits in sullen apathy to her wretched fate. This is the ordinary history of such cases.

Considering it unsafe to remain longer in this infected city, from the reports that the fever was gaining ground, I now made preparations for leaving New Orleans, and as I had made an engagement to manage the affairs of a gentleman in Florida, during his absence at Washington, I determined to proceed thither with the least possible delay. In furtherance of this object I made inquiries for a conveyance by water to St. Marks, giving the preference to steam. In this object I was, however, disappointed, and was obliged to take a passage on board a brig, about to sail for that obscure port. The vessel was towed down to the balize or mouth of the Mississippi, in company with two others, by a departing steamer, which had on board the mail for Bermuda and St. George's Island. Arrived at the balize, whose banks for several miles are overflowed by the sea, I saw a small fleet of vessels, some outward and some inward bound. Amongst these was a United States ship of war, of great beauty, carrying heavy guns. A boat from this vessel, in charge of an officer, boarded us, and delivered to the captain a sealed packet, which I understood to be a dispatch, addressed to General Taylor, the officer in command of the troops operating against the Indians in Florida.

The coast about the balize is low and swampy, and everywhere abounds in rush and cane brakes which give its sea-beach a desolate appearance. These morasses harbour thousands of alligators, whose roar had a singular effect as it rose above the breeze. Flocks of aquatic birds were to be seen on every side, the most numerous being the pelican, and a bird of the cotinga species, about the size of an English throstle, the plumage of which, being jet black and flamingo red, had a beautiful effect in the sunshine, as they flew or settled in thousands on the canes.

Our passage across the Gulf of Mexico was a favourable one, but when within forty miles of our destination, the vessel struck on a hidden sand-bank. The fog was so dense, that the captain had been mistaken in his reckoning, and had taken a wrong course. For a considerable time we were in great jeopardy, and every attempt to get the ship again afloat was unavailing; and, had not the weather been moderate, there is little doubt but that she would have been lost, and our lives placed in great peril. After some hours' exertion, during which an anchor was lost, and a quantity of iron thrown overboard, we had the satisfaction to find that the vessel was adrift.

This was a great relief to us, for had a gale sprung up in the night, which was closing in, we must have taken to the boat, and abandoned the vessel, a perilous undertaking, from which we all felt too happy to have escaped. I was told by the captain that the coast here abounds with hidden sand-banks of the description we had encountered. This, perhaps, together with the poor harbour accommodation in Florida, accounts for the small size of the vessels which generally trade there.

The desolate look of the coast from the deck of the vessel, did not convey to my mind a very favourable impression of the country, and the hostile disposition of the Indians tended not a little to excite forebodings of evil, that at one time almost induced me to abandon my intention, and return to the north. These apprehensions were, however, allayed by the representations of the captain of the vessel, who stated that the Indians seldom attempted to molest armed parties, and that an understanding with the government was daily expected, through the recent capture of some important sachems or chiefs, under whose influence and leadership hostilities had been carried on. This information reassured me, and I determined to proceed, although I found afterwards that it was almost entirely a misrepresentation, which, however, I cannot believe was wilful, as the captain would have had me for a passenger on the return voyage.

I soon after landed in a boat from the shore. The bay or harbour of St. Marks is not attractive, neither is the town, which presents a desolate appearance. The houses or stores are chiefly of wood, painted white, the venetian blinds of the houses being green, as in most parts of the United States. The hotel-entrances were crowded with loungers, in snow-white clothing, large Leghorn or palmetto hats, and fancy-coloured shirts, who smoked cigars incessantly, and generally discussed with energy the inroads of the Indians, or other leading topics of the day. The houses are low and irregularly built, and the appearance of the whole place and its inhabitants, as far as I could see, wore a forbidding aspect, and was indicative of anything but prosperity.

My next stage was to Tallahassee by railroad, through a desolate-looking country, whose soil was sand, and whose vegetation looked stunted, presenting little to cheer the senses, or call forth remark; in fact, everything around told of a country whose centre is flourishing, but whose frontiers are a wilderness. Just before we started, a well-dressed negro, apparently a footman or butler, applied for a seat in the carriage. He was told by the station-keeper, that there was no conveyance for "niggers" this train, and he must wait for the following one. He at first disputed his right to refuse him a passage in the carriage, which roused the ire of the station-keeper, who threatened to kick him if he was not soon off. This seemed to awe him, for he quietly left the station, muttering, however, as he went, his intention of reporting the circumstance to Colonel Gambole. This caused me to make some inquiry about the colonel whose name he had mentioned, and who I learned was his master. I was also informed that no negroes in that district were so insolent, owing to the indulgence with which all his hands were treated. I could see, however, that the negro had different men to deal with here, and if he had not taken his departure, he would, without a doubt, have been kicked or felled to the ground, on the least further provocation--a course pursued without hesitation in cases where a negro assumes anything like equality in the south.

CHAPTER V.

"The fragrant birch above him hung
Her tassels in the sky,
And many a vernal blossom sprung,
And nodded careless by.
But there was weeping far away;
And gentle eyes for him,
With watching many an anxious day,
Were sorrowful and dim."--BRYANT.

Florida, in which state I now found myself, is divided into East, West, and Middle. It is a wild extent of country, about 300 miles from north to south. The king of Spain held possession of the territory in 1810, but it was afterwards ceded by treaty to the Federal Government. It was discovered in 1497 by Sebastian Cabot. St. Augustine is the capital of East, and Pensacola of West, Florida. This country is, for the most part, a howling wilderness, and is never likely to become thickly populated. The dreary pine-barrens and sand-hills are slightly undulating, and are here and there thickly matted with palmetto.

In pursuance of my original design, I had now to penetrate nearly a hundred miles into the interior; and, as the Indians and fugitive negroes were scouring that part of the country in hostile bands, I contemplated this part of my route with no little anxiety. I determined, however, to proceed. The journey lay through a wild country, intersected with streams and rivers, every one of which swarmed with alligators. This, although not a very pleasant reflection, did not trouble me much, as I had by this time become acquainted with the propensities of these creatures, and knew that they were not given to attacking white men, unless provoked or wounded, although a negro or a dog is never safe within their reach. They are, however, repulsive-looking creatures, and it is not easy to divest the mind of apprehension when in their vicinity.

My destination was an inlet of the sea, called Deadman's Bay, from whence it was my intention, after transacting some business I had undertaken, to take passage by steamer to Cuba, intending to return to the continent, after a limited stay there, and on some of the adjacent islands. In this, however, I was disappointed, as I shall by-and-by show. My plan was to travel by easy stages under escort, and encamp out at night; so, having secured the services of six men, who were well armed and mounted on horseback, and having furnished ourselves with a tent and other necessaries, which were carried by individuals of the party, we left Tallahassee, on our way inland, under a scorching sun. We could proceed but slowly after reaching the pine-barrens, the soil of which is loose sand, and at every step the animals we rode sank to the fetlock, which caused them to be greatly fatigued at the close of the day.

At night-fall, after selecting our ground adjacent to a river, we pitched our tent, and supper was prepared. This consisted of jerked venison (dried by a slow fire), broiled turkey, two of which we had shot upon our way, bread, and coffee. One of our party walked round our position as a sentinel, and was relieved every two hours; it being necessary to keep a vigilant look out, on account of the Indian and runaway negro marauders, who roam through these wilds in bands, and subsist chiefly in plundering farms and small parties. A huge fire of resinous pine branches (which are plentiful in these solitudes, and strew the ground in all directions, blackened with fire and age) was blazing to keep off the wolves and catamounts, whose terrific yells, in conjunction with other beasts, prevented our sleeping. They did not, however, venture within rifle shot. The Indians, on attacking small parties, have a practice of imitating the cry of the wolf, and this circumstance being known to us, tended not a little to raise our suspicions on hearing the fearful howlings that rang through the wilderness.

In the morning, we proceeded through barren sand-plains, skirted with dense hammocks (jungles) and forests. We were much annoyed by mosquitoes and sandflies, which kept the whole party in discomfort from their attacks. Dusky-looking deer-flies constantly alighted on our faces and hands, and made us jump with the severity of their bites, as did also a large fly, of brilliant mazarine blue colour, about the size of a humble bee, the name of which I have forgotten.

In crossing one of the numerous streams, we had to wade or swim our horses over, an incident occurred which rather alarmed me. I was on a horse of that Arabian blood, build, and spirit, so common in saddle-horses in America, and a little in advance of the party, when I reached a river that intersected our track, and which we had to cross. After allowing the animal to quench its thirst, I applied spurs and urged it into the stream; it being averse from some cause to take the water. The stream was, however, deeper than I anticipated, and the horse immediately began to stumble and flounder in an alarming manner, showing that the river bed was uneven and rocky. About half-way across was a small island, that divided the stream, which after much difficulty he reached; resting here about a minute, I again urged him forward, but the animal seemed very reluctant to go. He wheeled short round, snorted loudly as if in fear, and was evidently in unusual alarm. After some coaxing, he, however, plunged into the water, and I expected to be able to gain the opposite shore in advance of my companions, but just as we were half-way between the little island and the opposite bank, which was very steep, the horse again became restive, rearing as if dreadfully frightened. I had the greatest difficulty to keep the saddle, which was a high Mexican one, covered with bear-skin, and as easy to ride in as a chair. I now began to suspect the cause of his alarm. The stream was one of those black-looking currents that flow noiselessly along, and which in Florida always harbour the largest-sized alligators. When I first came to it, I remembered this, and thinking to frighten off any of these lurkers that might be in the vicinity, I had dashed precipitately into the stream. This practice, or shouting loudly and firing a pistol into the water, usually succeeds. I soon found out, however, that the presence of one of the ugly creatures was the cause of the horse's trepidation, for, within six feet of us, I discerned a pair of eyes, set in huge brown excrescences, fixed intently on me and my horse, with malicious gaze. I knew they belonged to a veteran, and dreading lest its snout might be within two feet of my leg, for the old alligators boast enormous length of jaw, I sat tailor-wise in my saddle, and levelled my rifle at the horrid object; the reptile had, however, observed my movements, and disappeared beneath the surface; I instantly discharged my piece in the direction he had taken, and certainly gave him a lesson, for the water around me was directly after tinged with blood; he was probably hurt severely, or he might have resented my temerity. I soon after reached the shore in safety, where I was speedily joined by the escort, who saw nothing of the reptile in their way across, and who, being men bred amongst such scenes, and totally divested of fear, at once took the water, although they had witnessed the encounter.

The cayman of South America is very ferocious, and is popularly styled the hyena of the alligator tribe. This savage creature will instantly attack a man or a horse, and on this account the Indians of Chili, before wading a stream, take the precaution of using long poles, to ascertain its presence or to drive it away. Naturalists assert that the cayman is not found in the North American rivers, and I should imagine this to be correct, for, although engaged in many alligator hunts, I found from personal experience and minute inquiry that the species found in North America is harmless if unmolested.

After a laborious ride we arrived at Fort Andrews, where we found a military station of U.S. Infantry. We halted here for several days, I having business requiring my attention, and ourselves and our beasts needing to recruit our strength, before continuing our route to the Bay. The forest scenery here almost defies description. Immense cedars, and other lordly trees, rear their gigantic and lightning-scathed heads over their smaller and less hardy but graceful neighbours; cactuses, mimonias, and tropical shrubs and flowers, which at home are to be seen only in conservatories or green-houses are here in profusion,

> "And plants, at whose name the verse feels loath,
> Fill the place with a monstrous undergrowth,
> Prickly, and pulpous, and blistering, and blue,
> Livid, and starred with a lurid hue,"

while innumerable forms of insect and reptile life, from the tiny yellow scorpion to the murky alligator of eighteen feet in length, give a forbidding aspect to the scene. Racoons, squirrels, wild turkeys, pelicans, vultures, quails, doves, wild deer, opossums, chickmuncks, white foxes, wild cats, wolves,--are ever and anon to be seen among the high palmetto brakes, and the alligators in the bayous arid swamps, "make night hideous" with their discordant bellowings and the vile odour which they emit. The ***tout ensemble*** of the place brings to recollection those striking lines of Hood,

> "O'er all there hung the shadow of a fear,
> A sense of mystery the spirit daunted,
> And said, as plain as whisper in the ear,
> The place is haunted."

During my stay at Fort Andrews, a large detachment of U.S. troops arrived, continuing a campaign against the recreant Indians and negroes. The appearance of the men and officers was wretched in the extreme; they had for weeks been beating through swamps and hammocks, thickly matted with palmetto bush, which had torn their undress uniforms in tatters, searching for an invisible enemy, who, thoroughly acquainted with the everglades, defied every attempt at capture. The whole party looked harassed, disappointed, and forlorn. General Taylor was with and had command of this detachment, which was about 400 strong. As I had heard this man vauntingly spoken of in the north, as the brave cotemporary of Scott, I felt no little curiosity to see him. His appearance surprised me. He was a burly, unmilitary-looking man, of most forbidding aspect, and much more like a yeoman than a soldier. A sword, much out of place, dangled awkwardly by his side, and was the only badge of his profession about him, except a black leathern cap; otherwise, he was habited as a private citizen. His small army encamped below the fort; and, as I thought, in most un-general style, he superintended the erection of his own marquee. He had with him several negroes, who were his body servants; and the coarse epithets he applied to them during the operation did not prepossess me in his favour, or, I thought, reflect much credit on his refinement.

At nightfall cries of distress arose from the marquee, and as I approached it I could distinctly hear one of the bondsmen earnestly pleading for mercy. Listening for a moment, I heard this distinguished general exclaiming vociferously, and belabouring the poor negro heavily with a raw-hide whip; most likely venting the spleen he felt at his non-success against the Indians, the expedition having hitherto been unsuccessful. The poor negro had offended his master, by some trivial act, no doubt, and in southern style he was correcting him, without much regard, it is true, to publicity. This, in southern latitudes, is so common, that it is thought little of;

and the occurrence caused on this occasion only a passing remark from those present. The negro was his own, and he had a right, it was stated, to correct him, as and when he pleased; who could dispute it? For my own part, I entertained the most abhorrent feelings towards a man, who, without sense of shame, or decent regard for his station, thus unblushingly published his infamy amongst strangers, and this man a would-be patriot, too, and candidate for the Presidential chair, which, it will be remembered, he afterwards obtained. I was told that flogging his negroes was a favourite pastime with this eminently-distinguished general, and that he was by no means liked by his officers or men. His appearance bespoke his tyrannical disposition; and this, coupled with incapacity, there is little doubt, conduced to make it necessary for him to relinquish his command of the army of the south, which he did not long after, being succeeded, I believe, by General Armstead.

As I mentioned before, the force that accompanied him was in forlorn case, reminding me strongly of Shakspere's description of Falstaff's ragged regiment. It consisted chiefly of raw, undrilled troops, quite unused to discipline, but, perhaps, as effective as veterans in the service in which they were employed, the adroitness of the enemy, accustomed to the interminable swamps, hammocks, and canebrakes which abound in this country, quite paralyzing the energies of the men, and destroying that *esprit du corps* without which no success can be expected in an army.

Several Indian sachems or chiefs accompanied the command; these were fine-looking fellows, but appeared exhausted from long marching through the wilderness One of these, named Powell, particularly attracted my notice; he was a very interesting young man, of feminine aspect, and little resembling his stalwart companions. He had originally been captured, but by kind treatment had been brought over to friendly views, and was now acting as a guide. It was stated that his father was much incensed against him, and had employed emissaries to despatch him secretly. A few months after this campaign I heard that he was shot while out hunting; no doubt, at the instigation of his unnatural parent, who preferred his death to his continuing in league with white men.

Leaving Fort Andrews, I now pushed onward to Deadman's Bay. The country we passed through was much the same as I have before described; the journey took us the better part of two days. On the way we saw a herd of wild cattle, which scoured the plain in consternation on espying our party; urging on our horses, we tried to bring one down, but they outstripped us. Some miles farther on, and near a thick hammock, about a quarter of a mile a-head, a huge black bear stood snuffing the air; we again put spurs to our horses to try to intercept his retreat, but he was too quick for us, and made at his utmost speed (a sort of shambling trot) for the coppice or jungle, which he soon entered, and disappeared from our sight. At nightfall, a pack of ravenous wolves, headed by a large white one, serenaded us, and came near enough to our camp-fire to seize a small terrier belonging to one of the party. The poor animal, unused to the dangers around, had the temerity to run out and bark at the pack--he soon after gave one agonizing yelp, and we never saw him again. As a reprisal, three of the party fired, and brought one of the wolves to the ground; he was of great size, and, I should say, could have carried away a sheep, or a good sized hog (of which they are very fond), with ease. We could not, however, skin him--he was so infested with fleas. In the settlements they often seize and carry off children, but they do not molest adults.

As we proceeded, we kept a vigilant look-out for Indians, a number of whom, we had heard at Fort Andrews, had been driven in the direction we were travelling. We fortunately escaped molestation, but saw in several places human bones, probably the relics of a former combat between the United States troops, or travellers like ourselves, and Indians or negroes. One skull I picked up had been split with a tomahawk, besides having a bullet-hole in it about the region of the left ear. Our situation was one of great peril, but I had made up my mind to proceed at all hazards, despite the opposition shown by two or three of the settlers composing my escort, who, on more than one occasion, pointed out Indian camp-grounds of only a few days' age. At one of these we found a quantity of Indian flour or arrowroot, part of a bridle, and the offal of a calf; but we left the former, imagining it might be poisoned, the latter was of no use, our only dog having been devoured by the wolves. Passing through a dense hammock, of a quarter of a mile in width, through which the pioneers of the American army had recently cut a rough road, I dismounted, to take a view of these sombre shades on either hand. The solemn stillness around seemed to me like the shadow of death--especially so, from the peril we were in through the deadly feud existing at the time between the Indians and white men. I penetrated for full a quarter of a mile into this fastness in a lateral direction, and, in doing so, suddenly startled two immense white birds of the adjutant species, which were standing in a swamp surrounded by majestic cedar trees. I could easily have brought one down with my rifle, but I thought it wanton cruelty to do so. They were, I should think, quite six feet high, and beautifully white, with a yellow tinge. The head of one, which, I suppose, was the male bird, was surmounted by a golden crest. They sailed quietly away over my head, not appearing much alarmed by the intrusion.

In these primeval shades, where, perhaps, the foot of man never before trod (for I looked in vain for such traces), are many beasts, birds, and reptiles, which live in perfect security; for, although the Indian dwells here, and subsists by hunting, yet the territory is so vast, and the red men are so few in proportion, that there can be little doubt that many places are untraversed.

Emerging on the open sand-plain somewhat unexpectedly, I caused my party no little alarm; they instinctively grasped their rifles, imagining the approach of a party of hostile Indians.

The constant dread of molestation causes the traveller here to be ever on the *qui-vive*, the precaution being highly necessary, to prevent surprise. The least movement in a coppice excites apprehension, and fills the soul of both the resolute and the timorous with anticipations of danger. Nor are these fears groundless, for the treacherous Indian crawls stealthily to the attack, and, without a moment's warning, two or three of a party may fall to the earth, pierced by rifle-balls, or rearing horses may throw the riders, and leave them at the mercy of these ruthless assassins.

Arriving at length at the Bay in safety, I was accommodated in the officers' quarters of a temporary fort or stockade, erected there. The steamer had left, so that I was compelled to remain here longer than I had intended, awaiting the arrival of the next boat. To beguile the time, I went for miles into the forests, looking for game, often coming back disappointed and weary; at others rewarded by, perhaps, a racoon, or, what I valued more, a fawn or wild turkey. There was, however, plenty of sport on the river, and thousands of wild ducks, gannet, and pelicans, inhabited the little islands in the vicinity, and reared their young there; some of these islands being covered with their eggs. Large numbers of alligators infested the streams adjacent, and their bellowings, in concert with bull-frogs and other reptiles, often banished sleep for nights together, although I was pretty well accustomed to such annoyances. Snakes were often to be met with, although harmless if unmolested; amongst these, the moccason, hoop, and garter snakes, of which I procured several specimens, were the most common to be met with. Rattle-snakes exist in rocky districts, but I saw none of them here.

The steamer not arriving as I anticipated, after remaining for a considerable time, and getting tired of so solitary a life, I determined to retrace my steps to Tallahassee.

While remaining at this post, a party of mounted volunteers arrived from Georgia. These men were mostly sons of farmers, who had suffered from the unceasing attacks of the Indians on their farms, in many instances accompanied by the butchery of some members of their families. It was arranged that a company of U.S. Infantry, stationed at the fort, should act in concert with these men, and scour the country for twenty miles round, to search for Indians, traces of whom had been seen, and who, it was very certain, were encamped not many miles off. As I felt desirous of observing the operations of these little campaigns against so wily a foe, I intimated to a major, my intention of accompanying the expedition. He was pleased with the proposal, and furnished me with a splendid rifle and other equipments, from the stores of the depot. After a short delay, owing to the non-arrival of some waggons that were intended to accompany the expedition, the whole force mustered in front of the stockade enclosure, and being furnished with ten days' provisions for man and horse, started under command of the major aforesaid, across the sand-plains, in order to reach a dense cedar and cypress swamp, ten miles distant, where it was suspected the enemy was concealed. After a tedious march through a wild country, so overgrown with saw palmetto and underbrush, that our horses had great difficulty to get through it, we arrived at the skirts of the swamp; here a consultation took place between the officers present, and it was arranged that an Indian guide whom we had with us, should go in and hold a parley with the Indians, to induce them if possible, to surrender. The guide went into the hammock, which extended along the edge of the swamp as far as the eye could reach, right and left. I should have mentioned, that this man, with the usual Indian acuteness, had discovered indubitable signs that the enemy was in the vicinity, long before we reached the spot. After an absence of about an hour, during which time we refreshed ourselves, and made preparations for an expected struggle, our guide returned, bringing with him a bow and quiver of arrows, as proofs of his interview with the secreted Indians. The account he gave, which was interpreted by a half-bred Indian who accompanied the expedition for the purpose, was, that after penetrating some distance into the fastness, he came to the encampment of the enemy, and was instantly surrounded by warriors, who seized him, but after parleying for a considerable time, let him go, presenting him with a bow and arrows, as a symbol of their unflinching resolve to continue the war.

On hearing this, it was at once determined by the officer in command that the whole force (except a guard for the horses and waggons) should go in and surprise them. The guide shook his head at this, and, pointing towards the swamp, said, "That is the way. I have shown it to you; follow it if you will; I do not go." It was, however, of no use to dally, and orders were given for all hands to follow into the swamp. For my own part, I wished to stay behind, but was told that such a course was attended with danger, as the Indians would most likely emerge from another part of the hammock, and endeavour to seize the horses, and ransack the waggons. This decided my adopting the least of the two evils, although I fully expected we should have a battle. After penetrating for I should think upwards of two miles, sometimes up to our knees in miry clay, and often stopped by impassable barriers of wild vines and other prehensile plants, which annoyed us greatly, and made me regret a thousand times that I had courted such dangers and inconveniences, the sound of two rifle-shots threw the whole party into indescribable commotion. Supposing we were attacked, all hands flew as quick as thought to the trees around, where each one, peeping from behind the trunks which were sought as a shelter against the rifle-balls of the expected foe, waited for a few moments in great suspense, when, suddenly, a loud cheer from the party in advance, followed by several rifle-shots, told us they had come upon the encampment. As the firing ceased, I knew the Indians had fled; this seemed also the opinion of the volunteers near me, who simultaneously left their hiding-place, and pushed forward to the scene. On arriving at the spot, I found the soldiers around a large Indian fire, over which was suspended a boiling cauldron, filled with venison, the Indians having been, no doubt, preparing a meal when disturbed by us; by the side, and not far from the fire, was a large trough, made out of a fallen tree, in which was a quantity of arrowroot in course of preparation. This plant grows plentifully in this latitude, and is the principal fare of the Indians, their squaws superintending the management of it. The remains of a fine buck lay near, and also some moccasons, leggings, and other Indian gear.

The enemy we had so unceremoniously disturbed had, as usual, taken flight; but we found traces of blood, and the advanced party stated that they had fired on two warriors, who, with a woman and two children, were on the spot when they came up.

As it was deemed quite useless to pursue them, from their being, no doubt, well acquainted with the intricacies of the fastness, and, therefore, sure to evade us, we regaled ourselves on the venison, of which some refused to partake, lest it should be poisoned. It was decided that the force should emerge from the swamp to the open plain about a mile above the spot where we had left the waggons, by a circuitous route; this was accordingly done, but our progress was so difficult, that the Indians had ample opportunity to fly before us, and we saw no further traces of them.

On reaching the waggons, we found, to our great satisfaction, that all was safe, and as night was approaching, it was decided to encamp there, a spring of turbid water being in the vicinity A cordon of sentinels was accordingly placed around our resting-place, and some tents were pitched for a portion of the party; the remainder, wrapped in blankets, sleeping on the sand. After the whiskey had passed round, the jocular little major in command proposed a song, and as one of the infantry soldiers was an adept at the art, he was invited to our marquee. Although in the very midst of danger, for we knew not how formidable in number the Indians were, we passed a merry evening.

Soon after this affair, the party returned to the bay, and in a day or two I started on my return to Tallahassee. About twenty miles from Deadman's Bay, we overtook a fugitive negro, and as we came upon him unexpectedly, when turning the edge of a hammock, he had not time to retreat, being within rifle-range, or he would doubtless have done so. He threw up his arms, and gave a piercing shriek (an unvariable custom of Indians when in danger), expecting to be instantly shot. He had, however, nothing to fear, having fallen in with friends and not foes. As I saw he was without a rifle, I dashed forward and accosted him first. He was soon assured, by my manner of addressing him, and begged earnestly that we would not detain or hurt him. This I at once promised, if he would inform us whether Indians were near. He said no, they had left that country two suns (days) ago, taking an easterly direction, and we might proceed to Fort Andrews in safety.

After putting several other questions to him, I inquired if the Indians would cross our path to Tallahassee from that post. He said no, they were far off in another direction, having gone to East Florida, eighty miles distant. The fellow was in poor case, and begged for food, saying he was starving. I, therefore, desired the men to supply him with some dried venison and bread, which he ate with avidity. He refused to tell me his master's name, but said there were hundreds of negroes fighting with the Indians, six from the same plantation as himself. My companions were at first intent upon securing him, but being averse to that course, I dared them to do it; when, seeing I was fully determined on this point, they did not insist. Pointing to the hammock, after giving him a dram of brandy, I bid him be off, when he darted like a deer into the thicket, and disappeared from our view, with a loud shout of exultation.

About ten miles further on, as we passed the edge of a dense hammock, we heard the bay of an Indian dog, and fearing the proximity of a party of marauders, we were instantly on the alert. The dog did not, however, come out of the wood, and we rode from the dangerous vicinity with all dispatch. Arrived again at Fort Andrews, without any further adventure worth recording, we found a party of volunteers about to proceed to Fort Pleasant, in the direction we were going. After recruiting my now almost exhausted strength by a refreshing sleep, I went down to their encampment, by the river's edge. They had the day before encountered a strong party of Indians, whom they repulsed with loss. Some of the party showed me several bloody scalps of warriors they had killed. I could not help remarking the beauty of the hair, which was raven-black, and shone with a beautiful gloss. They had several captured Indian women with them, and half-a-dozen children; the former were absorbed in grief, and one in particular, whose young husband had been shot in the fray, and whose scalp was one of those I have just mentioned, was quite overwhelmed. The children, little conscious of the misery of their parents, swam about and dived in the river like amphitrites; they each carried a small bow and quiver of arrows. There is no doubt the Indians these volunteers had fallen in with and routed, were the identical party referred to by the negro we had met some forty-eight hours before.

I had made up my mind to stay at Fort Andrews for a time, partly to fulfil an engagement with a friend whom I had arranged to meet here, and to whom I shall shortly have to refer more at length, and partly to recruit my strength, a tertian ague having seized me, which much debilitated my frame, and made travelling very irksome. My accommodation was indifferent, but medical assistance, which I needed most, was not wanting, and I shall never forget the courtesy of the officers.

I employed my time chiefly in rambling the woods, when health would permit, and had a boat lent to me, with which, in company, I several times penetrated the tortuous river, Esteenahatchie, to the bay, some miles distant. At night the boats were all sunk, or they would have been stolen or destroyed by the Indians, who hovered round and committed petty depredations at every opportunity. Below the fort, was a ruinous mill, in a gloomy dell, through which the river wended its silent course. This had once been tenanted, but the inhabitants were murdered some years before by the Indians, who afterwards (as is their almost unvarying custom), added to the atrocity by setting fire to the building.

Sitting one day, after a lengthened ramble, in solitary meditation on my position and the surrounding scenery, I saw a fine Indian, who appeared greatly fatigued, emerge from the adjoining hammock, and walk to the edge of the stream, and there, after glancing round him with eager eye and air, he laid down his rifle, and stepping on to a tree which debouched into the stream (lying as it had been struck down by a tornado), he crouched down at the end of it, and commenced laving himself with the water. His appearance was romantic, and there is no doubt, from his dress, he was a warrior of some note, probably following his wife, one of the squaws captured by the volunteers I have before mentioned, and who were still at Fort Andrews, awaiting orders from General Taylor. I could have shot him to a certainty, had I been armed, which was not the case. Had it been so, however, I was predetermined never, unless in self-defence, to imbrue my hands in Indian or negro blood while in the territory, neither was I disposed to betray him, for I deeply sympathized with the misfortunes of his race, and well knew that an inexcusable spirit of aggrandizement on the part of the Federal Government had in the first place roused the indignation of both negroes and red men, and provoked hostilities. After performing his ablution, the Indian stalked like a deer into the recesses of the forest, I having in the mean time, as a matter of policy, moved out of danger, for he was no doubt animated with feelings of dire revenge, and in a very different mood from that in which I have described myself to have been at the time.

During my visit to Deadman's Bay, I had become acquainted with a Scotch gentleman, who was employed on the medical staff of the U.S. army, I believe, as a supernumerary, or candidate for a commission as a surgeon. He was a most agreeable companion, of good natural parts, fluent in conversation, intelligent in remark, free from egotism, and well educated, I believe, at Cambridge, in England. We soon became attached to each other. He accompanied me in my rambles, and we were almost inseparable companions during my stay. He was one of those beings, in fine, who seem to be sent at times to cheer the darkened highway of existence under gloomy circumstances; and I fondly hoped to enjoy with him a lengthened period of virtuous intimacy, and close, unalloyed friendship, on more propitious soil.

But the decrees of Providence are inscrutable, and "his ways," indeed, "past finding out." This was certainly strikingly exemplified by the catastrophe I am about to relate, which deprived me for ever of my friend.

When at the bay, he expressed a wish to visit St. Marks, Tallahassee, and Apalachicola, and stated his intention, as soon as his engagements permitted, to proceed thither by steamer, if opportunity offered--or failing this, to go overland, availing himself of some escort which might be proceeding in that direction. As I felt desirous to have his company, on my route to South Carolina, I arranged to halt at Fort Andrews, as before stated, that he should join me there in a week, and then proceed in company with me to Fort Pleasant, forty miles distant, and thence to Tallahassee.

The time having now come at which I was expecting his arrival, I was one morning anxiously looking out through the long vista of pine trees and barrens, when I descried in the distance two horsemen approaching at their greatest speed; I at first imagined them to be, as they indeed proved, an advanced party of my friend's escort--but, on their coming up, I could see, from the agitation they were in, and the foaming state of their horses, which were quite white and in a dreadfully exhausted state, that something alarming had happened.

The tale was soon told:--It appeared, that about midway between the two settlements, or stations, a party of Indians in ambush had fired upon the party, and my friend had been treacherously murdered. I was much affected by this intelligence, and, after some consultation with a gentleman there, determined to get up a pretty strong party, and proceed to the scene of the murder, to collect the remains of my poor friend, whose bones would otherwise be left, as I had seen others in those regions, to bleach on the sand hills. We soon started, the party consisting of fourteen men, well armed with rifles, bowie knives, and pistols, accompanied by a waggon, drawn by four stout mules and driven by a negro, to convey back the remains. The expedition was attended with no little danger, from the proximity of a newly-discovered party of Indians, who were committing dreadful ravages in the district--but whether in large or small force, was uncertain; they were, probably, the party I have before adverted to, lingering about the vicinity.

After a melancholy journey, during which we were so absorbed by our feelings, that little was said; we reached the fatal spot, it being pointed but by one of the party who formed my friend's escort.' It was on the edge of a dense hammock, by the skirts of which lay some enormous trees, which had been levelled by a recent tornado. From behind this barricade the Indians had unexpectedly fired on the party--the attack was so sudden, that they appeared to have been quite taken by surprise. This was the more extraordinary, as the whole neighbourhood was of a description likely to be chosen by the red men for an ambuscade. The party attacked must have been in great trepidation, for, from what I could glean, the survivors put spurs to their horses' flanks, and galloped off to Fort Andrews, leaving my poor friend entirely at the mercy of the enemy. The survivor, who accompanied us, stated, that they were riding in Indian file, as is customary there; that poor H---- was in front of him; and that, directly the Indians gave their fire, he saw him fall backwards from his horse, at the same time raising his left hand to his head. He could tell no more, the horse he was on having wheeled round suddenly, and been urged on in retreat by its rider, who was in the greatest imaginable terror. Had the party halted, and returned the fire, for they were well armed, in all probability some of the marauders would have been laid low, or, if the Indians were but few, they might at least have rescued my poor friend.

We found footmarks of Indians, which we traced; by these it appeared that they were in small force, and that when H---- fell from his horse he recovered his feet, and ran from the enemy, in the direction of the plain, for about two hundred yards--here it was evident he had been overtaken, and his skull cloven with a toma-hawk from behind. We soon discovered his remains in the sand, denuded of every particle of flesh and muscle by the vultures and the ravenous wolves. We collected the bones with reverential care, and placed them in the waggon, for transit to Fort Andrews.

On the bones of the little finger of the left hand was an emerald ring, which I had often seen the murdered man wear, and which, being covered with blood and sand at the time of the catastrophe, no doubt escaped the attention of the vil-lians who perpetrated the atrocious act. The left jaw was fractured by a rifle-bullet, which knocked him off his horse backwards, as described by one of the survivors.

In the pines opposite the place of ambush, we found several balls imbedded, and one had lodged in the pummel of the saddle of the man who was present, and who formed one of our party. It appeared probable that there were not more than four or five Indians engaged in the attack; a force which might easily have been repelled and annihilated with ordinary courage, but formidable enough to men wanting the presence of mind which is necessary under such circumstances.

After a fatiguing journey, for which I was at the time almost totally unfitted by ill-health, our party reached Fort Andrews, with the mangled remains of the victim. A short time afterwards these were committed to the sand, a military salute being fired over the grave by some soldiers at the garrison. On an elevated slab of wood, to the north of Fort Andrews, may be seen a zinc plate, erected by me to the memory of my friend, with his name, the date of his death, and an epitome of the circumstances attending it. This memento of regard has, in all probability, escaped the cupidity of the Indians, for I took the precaution to have it placed as much out of sight as possible, and the place of burial was off the beaten track.

Thus perished miserably, one whose generous openness and manly virtues ren-dered him dear to all who had the privilege of his acquaintance. He was a native of somewhere near Arbroath in Scotland, but his accent did not betray his nativity.

In traversing the sandy deserts of West Florida, I had frequent opportunities of tracing the devastating effects of those awful visitations in tropical climates--hurri-canes, or tornadoes; and, notwithstanding I had the good fortune to escape the dan-ger of being exposed to one, I more than once prepared for the worst. One of these was accompanied with phenomena so unusual and striking to a native of Europe, that I must not omit some notice of it, if for no other purpose than to convey to the mind of the reader one of the many unpleasant but wonderful accompaniments of a residence in these latitudes, so poetically, and indeed so truthfully, apostrophized as "the sunny south."

It was while on a journey (accompanied by two yeomen from East Florida, who were proceeding to join an expedition against the Indians to defend their hearths, and by the friend whose melancholy loss I have adverted to) from Deadman's Bay towards Tallahassee, that the occurrence I am about to mention took place It was in the height of summer, and for several days Fahrenheit's barometer had ranged from 84 to 90 degrees, the temperature being occasionally even higher, by some degrees, than this. We started soon after eight in the morning, and had ridden all day under a scorching sun, from the effects of which we were but ill-defended by our palm-leaf hats, for our heads were aching intensely--my own being, in common parlance, "ready to split," not an inapt simile, by the way, as I often experienced in the south. Towards evening, the sultriness increased to a great degree, and respiration became painful, from the closeness of the atmosphere. A suspicious lull soon after succeeded, and we momentarily expected the storm to overtake us. It was not, however, one that was to be relieved by an ordinary discharge of thunder, lightning, and rain--deeper causes being evidently at work. The denseness of the air was accompanied by a semi-darkness, similar to that which prevails during an eclipse of the sun, which luminary, on the occasion I refer to, after all day emitting a lurid glare, was so shrouded in vapour as to be scarcely discernible, even in outline--while a subterranean noise added to the terrors of our situation, which strongly called to mind the accounts we read of earthquakes and similar phenomena.

We moved slowly on, as people naturally would who were about to be overwhelmed in a calamity that threatened their annihilation, while an indefinable sensation of sleepiness and inertia seized the whole of the party. Vultures and other birds of prey screamed dismally, as they hovered round our heads in the greatest excitement, arising either from terror or the anticipation of a rich repast, we could not tell which. These voracious creatures, with great audacity, often descended to within a few feet of the heads of our horses, which seemed terror-stricken at their near approach. I took aim at one of the largest of them with my rifle, and it fell a little to my left, with an impetus I can only compare to the fall of a human being.

Directly it touched the ground, it vomited carrion and died. It was many feet in breadth from tip to tip of wing, but we were too perturbed to stop and measure it. When I discharged the rifle, the report was unusually faint, owing to the state of the air; so much so, that my companions, who were not fifty yards behind, scarcely heard it. The wild animals in the jungle which skirted the road, and which, in general, skulk in silence and secresy in their haunts, rent the air with their howlings. The very order of nature seemed about to be reversed, while the long streamers of grey moss swayed backwards and forwards mournfully from the trees, adding to the solemnity of the scene. As the party slowly wended its way through the wilderness, each individual looked round with suspicion, exchanging furtive glances, or now and then uttering some exclamation of alarm--their manner and bearing indicating minds ill at ease.

This dismal state of things lasted nearly an hour, after which time nature seemed to recover herself by a sudden throe, for a brisk breeze, which was highly refreshing to our senses, and which was attended by the loud hollow subterranean sound I have before referred to, unexpectedly sprang up, and swept off, as if by magic, the inertia of nature. What made the phenomenon more extraordinary, was the total absence of thunder or lightning. My companions shouted for joy when the hollow moan of the embryo tempest was heard to move off to the eastward (for, as they informed me, it told of deliverance from peril); I felt a sensation of delight I cannot describe, and heartily responded to the noisy demonstration of satisfaction raised by my companions.

Our horses, apparently participating in our delight, pricked up their ears, and snorted, fairly prancing with pleasure, tired and jaded as they were after thirty miles' travel through sand, into which they sank at every step fetlock deep, often groaning pitifully.

I noticed that, during the impending storm, they hung down their heads in a listless manner, and sighed heavily, a circumstance that to our minds presaged calamity, and which, I may add, was altogether unlike the usual indication of fatigue in animals which have travelled a great distance. Had the tornado burst upon us, instead of passing off as it did, it is very doubtful whether the hand that writes this would not have been mingled with its native dust, in the arid sands of Florida; for, as we rode on, we saw gigantic pine, cedar, and hiccory trees, torn up by the roots, and scattered over the surrounding country, by by-gone hurricanes, many of them hundreds of yards from the spot that nurtured their roots--while the gnarled branches lying across our track, scorched black-with the lightning, or from long exposure to a burning sun, impeded our advance, and made the journey anything but pleasant.

The occurrence I have mentioned formed a topic of conversation for some miles as we journeyed to our destination; and one of my companions stated, that a few months before, when in the neighbourhood of Pensacola, a hurricane came on unexpectedly, and caused great devastation, unroofing the houses, tearing up trees, and filling the air with branches and fragments of property. He happily escaped, although his little estate, situated at Mardyke Enclosure, some short distance from the town, was greatly injured, and some six or eight people were crushed to death by the falling trees and ruins of houses.

CHAPTER VI.

"Before us visions come
Of slave-ships on Virginia's coast,
Of mothers in their childless home,
Like Rachel, sorrowing o'er the lost;
The slave-gang scourged upon its way.
The bloodhound and his human prey."--WHITTIER.

Florida produces oranges, peaches, plums, a species of cocoa-nut, and musk and water-melons in abundance. The more open portions of the country are dotted over with clumps of gnarled pines, of a very resinous nature, white and red oak, hiccory, cedar, and cypress, and is in general scantily clad with thin grass, fit only for deer to browse upon. The dreary sameness of the interior of this desolate country is distressing to the traveller; and the journey from one settlement to another, through pine-forests, seems almost interminable.

One morning, a short time prior to my intended departure for Tallahassee, I was roused before daybreak by a rifle-shot, which was instantly followed by the cry of "Guard, turn out!" and much hubbub. As this was no unusual occurrence, from the constant apprehension we were in of an attack by the Indians on the stockade, and as it had several times occurred before during my stay, I resolved to lie and listen awhile before I rose. The earnest conversation and the noise of horses soon after satisfied me it was only a friendly arrival. I, however, felt anxious to obtain intelligence as to the success of a treaty then pending between the United States Government and the Indians; the favourable termination of which would not only render my return to Tallahassee more safe, but put a stop, perhaps for ever, to those constant scenes of blood and depredation that were by this time become quite sickening to me. This feeling was much enhanced at the time by the express between

Fort Andrews and Deadman's Bay, being shot by a party of the common enemy. The body of this poor fellow was never found, but traces of blood were to be seen near the spot where he had been attacked; and the saddle and bridle of his horse were found cut into a thousand pieces; the probability being that he was wounded and taken prisoner, doubtless to be tortured to death, a practice common with all Indian tribes in time of war.

On my proceeding to a house used as officers' quarters, outside the stockade, I found the stir had been caused by the arrival of two companies of light-horse soldiers from St. Marks, escorting several couples of bloodhounds, to aid the army, operating in that part of Florida, to exterminate the Indians. These dogs were very ferocious, and, on approaching the leashmen, who had them in charge, they opened in full yell, and attempted to break loose. The dogs had just arrived from Cuba with their keepers, their importation having been caused by the supposition, that, like the Maroons in Jamaica, who, for nearly thirty years, defied the colonists there, the Indians would be terrified into submission. This, however, turned out to be erroneous; for, on their first trial, the Indians killed several, and the scheme was very properly abandoned a short time after.

Such barbarous means were very unjustifiable, although many (to use the language of the Earl of Chatham, when deprecating a similar course in the English House of Lords) considered that every means that God and nature had placed in their hands, were allowable in the endeavour to bring to a close a war that had cost the Federal Government an immense amount of blood and treasure. I am of opinion, however, from what I afterwards heard, that the step was not an altogether popular one in the eastern and northern states, although it certainly was so in the southern; it being argued in the public prints there, that as dogs had been used in hunting down fugitive negroes from time immemorial, the mere fact of bloodhounds being used instead of mastiffs was a peccadillo unworthy of name.

The tobacco plant, though growing in many parts of Florida spontaneously, like the broad-leafed dock in England, is often cultivated in garden-ground for domestic use, some of the finer kinds being as aromatic as those of Cuba. The soil in such places is rich; indeed, the plant will not thrive in many parts where this is not the case. The method of propagation, generally followed by the large growers, is that recommended by Loudon, in his incomparable *Encyclopedia of Agriculture,* and is as follows:--The soil selected is in general loamy and deep; this is well broken up before planting, and frequently stirred to free it from the rich growth of weeds that, in Florida in particular, choke the growth of all plants if neglected. The seeds being small, they are lightly covered with earth, and then the surface is pressed down with a flat instrument used for the purpose. In two months after, the seedlings are ready to transplant, and are placed in drills, three feet apart every way. These are frequently watered, if there happens to be but little rain, which, in that arid climate, is often the case for weeks together, and the plants regularly looked over, to destroy a species of worm winch, if not removed, plays great havoc with the young buds. When four inches high, the plants are moulded up like potatoes in England; when they have six or seven leaves, and are just putting out a stalk, the top is nipped off, to make the leaves stronger and more robust. After this, the buds, which show themselves at the joints of the leaves, are plucked, and then the plants are daily examined, to destroy a caterpillar, of a singular form and grey in colour, which makes its appearance at this stage, and is very destructive to narcotic plants. When fit for cutting, which is known by the brittleness of the leaves, the plants are cut close to the ground, and allowed to lie some time. They are then put in farm-houses, in the chimney-corner, to dry; or, if the crop is extensive, the plants are hung upon lines in a drying-house, so managed that they will not touch each other. In this state, they are left to sweat and dry. When this takes place, the leaves are stripped off and tied in bundles; these are put in heaps, and covered with a sort of matting, made from the cotton-fibre or seaweed, to engender a certain heat to ripen the aroma, care being taken lest a fermentation should occur, which injures the value of the article; to avoid which the bundles are exposed and spread about now and then in the open air. This operation is called ventilating by the planters, and is continued until there is no apparent heat in the heaps. The plant is quite ornamental, and its blossoms form a pleasing feature in a garden of exotic productions.

After a brief stay at Fort Andrews, subsequent to the last sad offices for my deceased friend, I left that spot on horseback for Tallahassee, in company with four settlers. We soon reached the more populated districts, without being molested by the Indians. Here they had committed sad devastations; we saw many farms without occupants, the holders having been either murdered by midnight assassins, or having fled in alarm. Adjoining these habitations, we found line peach orchards, teeming with fruit of the richest description, which lay in bushels on the ground, and with which we regaled ourselves. Enclosed maize fields overgrown with brambles, and cotton fields with the gins and apparatus for packing the produce in bales for the market, presented to the eye the very picture of desolation.

Owing to cross roads we were at one time completely at fault, and there being no house in sight, I volunteered to ride off to the right and endeavour to obtain the information we were in need of. After riding about half-a-mile, I heard voices through a road-side coppice, which I took to be those of field-hands at work; going farther on I dismounted, and climbing the zigzag rail fence approached a negro at work in the field. I inquired if he could put me on the road to Tallahassee; he appeared much frightened at the intrusion, but stated he did not know, but his mas'r did, at the same time pointing to the plantation-house, situate the greater part of a mile distant; being averse to going there, for fear of impudent interrogation, I offered him money to go with me to the point where I had left my companions, and show us the way to the next house; he did not even know what it was I offered him, and in apparent amazement inquired what that was for; I explained, buy tobacco, buy whiskey; he appeared totally ignorant of its use, and I have no doubt he had never had money in his possession, or learned its use. Still, he refused to leave the field, a wise precaution, as I afterwards found, both for himself and me. The negro being resolute, there was now no alternative but to go to the house, on arriving at which, I met with such a reception as I had feared and anticipated. Three fierce dogs of the mastiff breed, regularly trained to hunting fugitive negroes, rushed out upon me. I had only a small riding whip with me, having left my fire-arms with a friend at Fort Andrews, and much dreaded laceration. Their noise soon brought out a ferocious, lank-visaged-looking man, about forty years of age, who immediately called off the dogs; but before I had time to make the inquiry that brought me there, he began in about the following strain,

"What dye yer waunt up yar, stranger? Arter no good, I guess; you'd better put it 'bout straight. I see'd yer torking to the hands yonder--none o' yer 'mancipator doctrines yar."

The fellow's address "struck me all of a heap," as he would himself have said, had he been in my situation; he spoke so fast, that I could not edge in a word; at last I stated the cause of my intrusion, but he would not believe a word, ordered me to quit the plantation or he would set the dogs on me, and was getting into such an ungovernable rage, that I thought it would be wise to follow his advice. So I slowly retreated to the yard entrance by which I had come in. Returning to my companions at the cross-roads, I found that, in my absence, a passer-by had given them the wished-for information, and we pushed on to a house of call, a few miles distant.

As the ride was a long one, we halted at this house for refreshment, and, after baiting our horses, regaled ourselves upon some choice ham and eggs. At the table, three little negroes, one girl and two boys, under fourteen years of age, served as waiters. Their clothing was supplied by nature, being solely the primitive habiliments worn in Eden before the fall. This is quite customary in the south, where the rules of decency are commonly set at defiance, as if the curse of Adam's transgression applied not in this respect to the African race. The little creatures did not seem to be in the least aware of their degraded state; they were as agile as fawns, and their tact in administering to the wants of the company was quite remarkable.

Just as we were about to proceed on our journey, a party of some half-a-dozen planters or overseers of neighbouring estates, mounted on fine mules, who had been searching for fugitive field-hands, rode up. I could see they were greatly excited, and one of them had a negro lassoed by the neck, one end of the rope being fastened to his high Spanish saddle. On coming up to the entrance gate, the one most in advance dismounted to open it; the mule, eager, perhaps, to get to a crib, or, what is more likely, to evade a brutal kick or blow, trotted through; this did not please its owner, who bellowed loudly to it to stop. The mule, however, still kept on, when the ruffian, in demoniac anger, drew from his belt a long bowie knife, and darting after the animal, hurled it at him with all his force. The blade of the weapon, which was six or seven inches long, entered and stuck fast in the abdomen of the agonized creature, which, for about twenty yards, ran on furiously, with the murderous knife in its vitals. It then fell-with a deep groan, while the fiend who had perpetrated this wanton act of barbarity and his companions watched its fall, and loudly exulted in it. I noticed that there was a deep scowl of hatred on the countenance of the negro prisoner as this drama was being enacted, and when the knife struck the poor mule he cried out, "Oh, mas'r, mas'r!" Societies for the suppression of cruelty to animals, are, as might be supposed, unknown in such remote situations, nor do they exist in any of the slave States and territories of America; so that redress in such a case was out of the question. I therefore consoled myself that the outrage had brought its own punishment in the loss of the mule, which was at least worth from eighty to one hundred dollars.

Passing onwards, we reached Tallahassee by rather a circuitous route, *via* Mount Pleasant. Although in an indifferent state of health, from exposure to the poisonous miasma of the country, I, on the whole, felt pleased with my journey, now that its dangers were over, and grateful to the great Dispenser of all good, who had safely conducted me through them. At Tallahassee I saw in the streets, in charge of a ruffianly-looking fellow, two negroes, with heavy iron collars round their necks. These were captured run-aways; the collars, which must have weighed seven or ten pounds, had spikes projecting on either side. One of the poor creatures had hold of the spikes as he walked along to ease the load that pressed painfully on his shoulders.

General Murat resided at the time in this neighbourhood; he is the brother of Jehoiachin, ex-king of Naples, and owns a large plantation, and, I was told, upwards of two hundred negroes, who were described as being humanely treated by him. This, however, is a very indefinite term, where all slave-owners profess to do the same, though the poor wretches over whom by law they impiously assume God's heritage, in ninety cases out of every hundred, are scantily clothed, worse fed than horses or mules, and worked to the utmost extent of human endurance, the humanity being, in most cases, left to the tender mercies of a brutal overseer, who exacts all he can. If the poor, tattered, squalid-looking beings I saw in Tallahassee be a fair specimen of the "humane treatment" I have referred to, heaven help them.

General Murat, some years ago, married an American lady, who delighted in being called the "princess," a little piece of vanity quite in keeping with the aristocratical prejudices of American females in the south, who are devoted worshippers of lordly institutions and usages. I did not see the general myself, but was told he was often to be met lounging about the bars of the principal hotels (being quite Americanized in this respect). He was described as a very garrulous old gentleman, extremely fond of recounting his adventures, particularly his escape when the allied troops entered Paris, about the year of Bonaparte's subjugation.

After remaining a few days in Tallahassee, I took the conveyance to Macon in Georgia, intending to pursue my route overland to Charleston in South Carolina. In the diligence (a clumsy apology for a coach) from Tallahassee to Macon, were several loquacious passengers. One of these amused and disgusted us by turns; for, after giving an epitome of his career, which was a chequered one, he related an incident that had recently occurred on a plantation he had been visiting, and, as it presents a novel feature in the asserted rights of slave-holders--how profane, I will not stop to inquire--I think it worth recording. After a recital of a drunken debauch, in which he had taken a part, described by him as a frolic, and which had been kept up for several days, his host, he said, anxious to show the high sense he entertained of the honour of the visit by making almost any sacrifice (this was said with great conceit), proposed to put a negro up with an apple on his head, in imitation of the ordeal imposed on William Tell, the Swiss patriot, declaring that he who divided the apple, or perforated it with a rifle-ball, should own the slave. This proposal, the gentleman very facetiously observed, the party jumped at, expecting some good sport; but added, "The fellow spoilt it, for he refused to stand still, although we 'used up' a cowhide over him for his obstinacy." The frivolous manner in which this intended outrage was related, filled me and my fellow-passengers with disgust. I thought it was not safe to remark on the proceeding, for I could see he was a very strenuous upholder of that disgraceful system of oppression, which stigmatizes and degrades the Americans as a people, and will continue to do so, until it is utterly abrogated, and their characters retrieved.

This would-be patrician was a pedantic, swaggering bully, who, it was evident, entertained high notions of his importance, and owned, perhaps, large possessions,--in a word, he was an American aristocrat, and the description I have given is a fair one of his class in the south. Pointing to a hill, as we entered a little settlement on our way to Macon, he exclaimed, "See there, gentlemen, twenty years ago I toiled up that hill without a cent in my wallet (purse), but now" he continued, with the air of a potentate, "my niggers are the sleekest in our country. In those days," he went on, "glass inkstands stood on the desks of the bank I now am chief proprietor of; we have nothing but gold ones now." The fellow's bombast lowered him in the esteem of the passengers, who seemed indisposed to listen to him, and the latter part of the journey he said little, being in fact regularly sent to Coventry by us all. He afterwards amused himself much to our annoyance by whistling airs and singing snatches of songs, which caused one of the passengers, a lady, to leave the diligence at the next change of horses. He was quite an adept at whistling the air of "Yankee doodle." This want of deference to the sex, which I must say is an exception to the general behaviour of men there and in other parts of the Union I visited, did not fail to call forth animadversion; the remarks at one time being so pointed, that I began to feel uneasy lest the pugnacious spirit might be aroused in him, which leads so often in the south to serious encounters.

Our conveyance, which more resembled a waggon than, a stage-coach, having by this time stopped at a large hotel at Macon, I alighted with much pleasure, for the roughness of the road, the disagreeable loquacity of the passenger I have described, and the recklessness of the driver, made the journey excessively unpleasant.

The negro population in Georgia is very numerous, and their constant attempts to escape to the everglades in Florida, make unceasing vigilance on the part of their owners necessary for the safety of their property. In many instances where suspicion exists, they are never allowed on any pretence, to leave the estate or residence of the owner.

At the Greensborough Railway Terminus, I noticed two negroes on their way to Charleston. Before being allowed to take their seat in an open carriage in the rear of the train, the clerk at the station stepped up to them, and with an air of great effrontery demanded to see their passes; these were instantly shown with an alacrity that plainly indicated fear; they were then shut in a box in the rear of the train, in which I could see no sitting accommodation. The way in which these men were treated presented nothing new, for I had invariably noticed that coloured people in the south, whether bond or free, were spoken to with supercilious haughtiness, which I never once saw them openly resent.

On arriving at the next station a trader got into the carriage. He had with him two negro men and a boy; these were secured to each other by hand-cuffs and a slight negro chain.

For the last forty miles of my journey, I had a very pleasant companion in a gentleman from the state of Alabama. He was a most agreeable and intelligent young fellow, but invalided like myself through the poisonous miasma of the south. I entered freely into conversation with him on general matters, in the course of which I introduced slavery in several of its bearings. I soon discovered by his bias, that he was decidedly in favour of "things as they are."

Being anxious to obtain some information as to the observance of the nuptial tie amongst slaves, I touched upon that subject, when he told me the ceremony was mostly a burlesque, and that unions were in general but temporary, although he had known some very devoted couples. But he proceeded to state that there was much room for reform in this respect. "I will relate to you an instance," said he, "of the manner in which this, as we white people consider it, solemn compact, is entered into amongst field-hands. When a couple wish to live together as man and wife, the male nigger mentions it to the overseer, and if there are no impediments, they have a cabin assigned to them." He described a scene of this kind, which I will endeavour to give verbatim. He said it occurred on his father's estate, some years before, and that he was standing by at the time, "although," he continued, "'tis done the same now in most instances." A negro approached where the overseer was standing, apparently, by his sidling manner, about to ask some favour, when the following colloquy ensued.

Overseer.--Well, you black rascal, what do you stand grinning there for?

Negro.--Please, mas'r, want Lucy for wife.

Overseer.--Wife, you scoundrel, what do you want a wife for; be off with you, and mind your horses. (He was employed as a teamster on the estate.)

Negro.--Oh, mas'r, I loves Lucy.

Overseer.--And she loves you, I suppose. A fine taste she must have, indeed. Where are you going to live?

Negro--Got room in No. 2 cabin, if mas'r please let 'um.

Overseer.--Well, now listen; go along, and take her, but, you lazy dog, if you get into any scrapes, and don't work like live coals, I'll send her to the other estate (which was situated forty miles distant), and flay you alive into the bargain.

The poor fellow, after thanking the overseer (not for his politeness, certainly), darted off to communicate the joyful intelligence to his affianced, making the welkin ring with his shouts. The gentleman who described this scene said that it was always the custom on his father's estate to give a gallon or two of whiskey for the attendant merry-making.

After numerous stoppages, the train at length reached Charleston. The journey from Greensborough had been a tedious one; besides the annoyance of slow travelling, through the inefficient state of the line, which was so defective that the carriages frequently left the rails, the noisome effluvia arising from the swamps we had to pass through, which harbour innumerable alligators and other reptiles, had the most debilitating effect on the frame, which was increased by the extreme sultriness of the weather After leaving my ticket at the terminus, I disposed of my baggage by hiring a negro to carry it to my boarding-house, and slowly wended my way into the city. A spacious public square at the end of King-street, through which I had to pass to my ***table d'hote***, presented an animated view, the citizens being assembled to celebrate the anniversary of the Independence conferred by Washington and his compatriots by the solemn declaration of the 4th July, 1776. Long tables, under gay awnings, to shield the company from the burning rays of the sun, which at the time were intense, groaned with every luxury the climate afforded; but the banquet was not furnished by this alone, for Cuba and some of the neighbouring islands, it was stated, had been ransacked for delicacies. Crowds of elegantly-dressed ladies (in general of very sallow look and languid air) and spirit-like children, with swarthy-looking men, many of whose visages bore evident traces of exposure to the ill effects of the climate and of dissipation, crowded the festive board. The negro attendants in dozens moved about with automatic order, as is characteristic of all the race on such occasions, for the negro is a "model waiter" at a banquet. Their snowy costumes contrasting strongly with their black visages and the jovial scene around. The merry peals of laughter, as some unlucky wight upset a dish, or scattered the sauce in everybody's face within reach, indicated lightness of heart, and merriment and conviviality seemed the order of the day.

The imposing scene before me, after a long absence from social meetings in civilized life, was very cheering, and, had it not been for the inertia I felt at the time, arising from a fatiguing journey and the tertian ague, I should have felt disposed to participate in the day's enjoyment. Other considerations might, however, have prevented this: I was a stranger to all around, and knew that I should be either subjected to impertinent interrogations, or become the object of invidious remark--this, in my debilitated state of health, I felt anxious to avoid, as calculated to impede my restoration. My joining the assembled party might also have involved the chance of surveillance during my stay, which, before my departure for Europe, I intended should be rather protracted. I may have been mistaken in this view, but, from the character I had heard of the place, I felt justified in giving way to the suspicion.

I was beguiled into the erroneous idea that a sense of happiness and security reigned in the assembled multitude, a notion quite fallacious, from attendant circumstances, as I shall directly explain. Troops were stationed at a guard-house in the vicinity, and the sentinels paced in front of the building, as if in preparation for, or in expectation of, a foe, affording a great contrast to the apparent security of the inhabitants assembled in the square. Before reaching Charleston, I had been apprised of the state of jeopardy the citizens were in from the possibility of a recurrence of those scenes of anarchy enacted at the insurrection of the slaves some time before--scenes which had filled every heart with dismay, and spread ruin and desolation on every side. From what I could glean of that fearful drama, the slaves in the surrounding districts, on a concerted signal from their confederates in Charleston, made a descent upon the city, and, rendered furious by long oppression, proceeded to fire it and massacre the inhabitants. No language can convey an accurate idea of the consternation of the white inhabitants, as it was described to me. The tocsin was sounded, the citizens assembled, armed *cap-a-pie*, and after much hard fighting, the rebellion was crushed, and large numbers of the insurgents were slain or arrested. Then came the bloody hand of what was impiously termed retributive justice. A court, or sort of drum-head court-martial, not worthy to be called a trial, condemned numbers of the slaves to death, and they were led out instantly to execution. My informant told me that many a brave, noble-hearted fellow was sacrificed, who, under happier circumstances, though in a cause not half so righteous, would have been extolled as a hero, and bowed down with honours. Many a humble hearth was made desolate, and, in the language quoted by my informant, "as in the days of the curse that descended on the people of the obdurate Pharaoh, every house mourned its dead." Still, there was a strong lurking suspicion that the *emeute* of the negroes had only been temporarily suppressed, and awful forebodings of fire and of blood spread a gloom on the minds of all. This was the version given to me by a friend, of what he described as the most fearful rising amongst the negroes ever before known in the southern states of America.

As I passed up the long range of tables, the health of the President of the Republic was responded to by the company. The cheers were deafening, and, what most surprised me was, that the negro waiters joined heartily, I may say frantically, in it, and danced about like mad creatures, waving their napkins, and shouting with energy. Some of the elder ones, I noticed, looked mournfully on, and were evidently not in a gay humour, seeming a prey to bitter reflections. Notwithstanding the curse of slavery, which, like a poisonous upas, taints the very air they breathe with the murdered remains of its victims, the white citizens of the south are extremely sensitive of their civil and political rights, and seem to regard the palladium of independence secured by their progenitors as an especial benefit conferred by the Deity for their good in particular. Actuated by this mock patriotism (for it is nothing less), the citizens of the south omit no opportunity of demonstrating the blessings they so undeservedly inherit, and which, if I am not mistaken, will, ere many years elapse, be wrested from them, amidst the terrible thunders of an oppressed and patient people, whose powers of endurance are indeed surprising.

Leaving the square, I passed up King-street, at the top of which was my intended boarding-house. The shops in this fashionable resort are fitted out in good style, and the goods are of the best description. After sunset the streets are often lined with carriages. The city lies flat, like the surrounding country, and, owing to this, is insalubrious; stagnant water collects in the cellars of the houses, and engenders a poisonous vapour, which is a fertile source of those destructive epidemics, that, combined with other causes, are annually decimating the white population of the south of the American continent in all parts.

At the top of King-street, facing you as you advance, is a large Protestant episcopal church. I went there to worship on the following Sunday, but was obliged to leave the building, there being, it was stated by the apparitor, no accommodation for strangers, a piece of illiberality that I considered very much in keeping with the slave-holding opinions of the worshippers who attend it. This want of politeness I was not, however, surprised at, for it is notorious, as has been before observed by an able writer, that, excepting the Church of Rome, "the members of the unestablished Church of England--the Protestant Episcopalian, are the most bigotted, sectarian, and illiberal, in the United States of America. Being fully persuaded," to follow the same writer, "that prelatical ordination and the three orders are indispensable to their profession, they are, like too many of their fellow professors in the mother country, deeply dyed with Laudean principles, or that love of formula in religion and grasping for power which has so conspicuously shown itself among the Oxford tractarians, and which, it is to be feared, is gradually undermining Protestant conformity, by gnawing at its very heart, in the colleges of Great Britain." Vital piety, or that deep sense of religious duty that impels men to avoid the devious paths of sin, and to live "near to God," is, I am inclined to believe (and I regret it, as a painful truth), by no means common in America. There are, however, many pastors who faithfully warn their flocks of the dangers of the world, and who strenuously advise their hearers to take warning lest they be over-captivated with the "Song of the Syrens." These, however, I must say, are chiefly in the free states, for I cannot regard southern ministers in any other light than pharisaical, while they continue openly (as is their constant practice) to support from their pulpits the institution that is the main stay of the southern states; I mean slavery. In my intercourse with serious individuals with whom I came in contact during my stay on the continent of America, the doctrines of Dr. Pusey and his confederates were often referred to; and although I believe "the Association for restoring the ancient powers of the Clergy, and the primary rites and usages of the Church," does not acknowledge the Protestant Episcopalians in America (owing, perhaps, chiefly to the invidious position the latter stand in with the state, and the little chance of their views being universally embraced by them, but partially, no doubt, to the evangelical principles of most of the ministers officiating in that Church), yet the subject has excited much interest there, and the Romish propensities of many pastors plainly indicate that inherent love of power that invariably, and, it may be said, necessarily, developes itself in hierarchical institutions--a propensity that ought to be closely watched by Protestant lay congregations, as being not only innovating and dangerous in its tendency, but calculated to foster that superstition which is at once the fundamental principle of the faith of the city of the seven hills, and the power of that triple-crowned monster, Popery.

I afterwards went into a large Independent chapel in another part of the town, where I was more courteously treated. Here was a very eloquent and noted preacher, a Dr. Groyard, from Mobile. He was delivering a very eloquent harangue, interspersed with touches of pro-slavery, sentimentalism and rhetorical flourish, the former especially directed to the negroes in the gallery, when, suddenly, a cry of "Fire! fire!" was raised in the street. The learned Doctor stood as if electrified, and the instant after his hearers rushed pell-mell out of the chapel, amidst the shrieks of the females, and the consternation of the men, caused, without doubt, by a lurking suspicion of impending evil from the negroes which I have before referred to. On ascertaining that the alarm was caused by a house being on fire in the vicinity, the service was abruptly terminated.

The following day I continued my perambulations; to the left of the episcopal church I have already mentioned, and surrounded by umbrageous trees in a park-like enclosure, is the Town-hall. I entered this building, where I found a bench of magistrates, the mayor of the city being amongst them, adjudicating on the cases brought before them. These consisted chiefly of negroes apprehended in the streets after nine o'clock the previous night; they were in all cases, except where their owners paid the fine, sentenced to receive from ten to twenty lashes, which were administered at once by the city gaoler, in a yard at the rear of a building, near which officers were in attendance for the purpose. I must mention, in explanation, that one of the laws passed directly after the insurrection, was to prohibit negroes, on any pretence, to be out after nine, p.m. At that hour, the city guard, armed with muskets and bayonets, patrolled the streets, and apprehended every negro, male or female, they found abroad. It was a stirring scene, when the drums beat at the guard-house in the public square I have before described, preparatory to the rounds of the soldiers, to witness the negroes scouring the streets in all directions, to get to their places of abode, many of them in great trepidation, uttering ejaculations of terror as they ran. This was an inexorable law, and punishment or fine was sure to follow its dereliction, no excuse being available, and as the owners seldom submitted to pay the fine, the slaves were compelled to take the consequences, which, in the language that consigned them to the cruel infliction, "consisted of from ten to twenty lashes, well laid on with a raw-hide," a murderous whip, which draws blood after the first few strokes, and is as torturing, I should imagine, as the Russian knout, certainly proving in many instances as fatal as that odious instrument. The crowning severity of the enactments I have referred to, remains, however, to be told. So heinous in a negro, is the crime of lifting his hand in opposition to a white man in South Carolina, that the law adjudges that the offending member shall be forfeited. This is, or was, quite as inexorable as the one I have before spoken of, and when in Charleston, I frequently, amongst the flocks of negroes passing and repassing, saw individuals with one hand only. Like the administration of miscalled justice on negroes in all slave-holding states in America, the process was summary; the offender was arrested, brought before the bench of sitting magistrates, and on the ***ex parte***[1] statement of his accuser, condemned to mutilation, being at once marched out to the rear of the building and the hand lopped off on a block fixed there for the purpose. I noticed a block and axe myself in the yard of a building near the town-hall, and on looking at them closely, saw they were stained almost black, with what I have little hesitation in saying was human blood. My conductor, however, tried to divert my attention from the object, and knowing I was an Englishman, refused to enter on the subject.

Another of the many cruel laws put in force after the ***emeute*** of the negroes, was to prohibit any coloured person from walking on the pavements, and forcing all males to salute every white they met. These distinctions, although falling into disuse, are not even yet abolished, but still, with many others equally odious, disgrace the Carolinean statute book. I saw several negroes from the plantation districts, walking in the road instead of on the pavement, in accordance with this law, touching their hats to every white passer-by; they were consequently obliged to be continually lifting their hands to their heads, for they passed white people at every step. Although I believe no punishment is now enforced for the omission of this humiliating homage to colour, the men I have referred to were doubtless afraid to disregard the ceremony.

A partiality exists in every part of America for music; indeed, so strongly is this developed, that in almost all the towns, and even in some hamlets in the western states, subscription bands are kept up--these play every evening, when the weather admits, in the centre of the public square, the citizens the while promenading round with their wives and families.

But, although a decided penchant prevails for music, the preference is given by the mass to a few ordinary airs, calculated to inspire that love of country which every reminiscence of the struggle for independence calls forth. The favourite air is the so-called national one of "Hail, Columbia," although this is but second to the fantastic drollery of "Yankee Doodle;" the latter is vociferously called for at all places of amusement, and excites in the audience, at such places of resort, almost frantic sensations. This is the more remarkable, as it was originally composed by an Englishman, and, as it is so intimately connected with Americanism, I shall, per-

---

1   The writer was assured, when in Charleston, that this was the case in five out of every six cases.

haps, be excused for introducing here what may be termed its history.

In the attacks made upon the French posts in America, in 1755, those against Niagara and Frontenac were made by Governor Shirley, of Massachusetts, and General Jackson, of New York. Their army during the summer lay on the eastern bank of the Hudson, a little south of Albany. Early in June, the troops of the eastern provinces began to pour in company after company, and such an assemblage never before thronged together on such an occasion. "It would have relaxed the gravity of an anchorite," says the historian, "to see the descendants of the Puritans marching through the streets of the ancient city, and taking their stations on the left of the British army--some with long coats, and others with no coats at all, and with colours as various as the rainbow; some with their hair cropped like the army of Cromwell, and others with wigs, the locks of which floated with grace round their shoulders. Their march, their accoutrements, and the whole arrangement of the troops, furnished matter of amusement to the British army. The music played the airs of two centuries ago; and the ***tout ensemble***, upon the whole, exhibited a sight to the wondering strangers to which they had been unaccustomed."

Among the club of wits that belonged to the British army, there was a Doctor Shackburg attached to the staff, who combined with his knowledge of surgery the skill and talent of a musician. To please the new-comers, he composed a tune, and, with much gravity, recommended it to the officers as one of the most celebrated airs of martial music. The joke took, to the no small amusement of the British. Brother Jonathan exclaimed, it was "nation fine;" and in a few days, nothing was heard in the provincial camp but the air of "Yankee Doodle."

Little did the author, in his composition, then suppose, that an air, made for the purpose of levity and ridicule, should be marked for such high destinies. In twenty years from that time, the national march--now universally recognized by the patriots--inspired the heroes of Bunker's Hill; and, in less than thirty, Lord Cornwallis and his army marched into the American lines to the tune of "Yankee Doodle."

CHAPTER VII.

"Woe worth the hour when it is crime
To plead the poor dumb bondman's cause,
When all that makes the heart sublime,
The glorious throbs that conquer time,
Are traitors to our cruel laws."--LOWELL

The general appearance of the majority of the coloured people in the streets of Charleston denoted abject fear and timidity, some of them as I passed looking with servile dread at me (as they did at almost every one who happened to pass), so that I could read in many of their looks a suspicion of interference, which, commiserating their condition as I did, was quite distressing.

It is impossible to form a correct estimate of what the perpetuators of slavery have to expect, if once the coloured population obtain a dominant position. The acknowledged gradual depopulation of the whites in the slave states, through sickness, exhaustion of the land, and consequent emigration, united with other causes, there is no doubt will eventually result in a great preponderance of coloured people, who, aroused by the iniquitous treatment they undergo, will rise under some resolute leader, and redress their wrongs. I was quite struck to see in Charleston such a disproportion of the colours, and, without exaggerating, I can say, that almost if not quite three-fourths of those I met in the streets were, if not actually of the negro race, tinged in a greater or less degree with the hue.

Pursuing my perambulations, I came to the slave and general cotton place of vendue, to the left of the General Post-office, which building is a very substantial edifice of stone. Here a dozen or twenty auctioneers were loudly holding forth to the assembled crowds, and cracking up their wares in New York style. The most indescribable scene of bustle and confusion prevailed, the whole street being covered with open bales and boxes of goods. In one part of the street was a slave warehouse, and advertisements were placarded outside of the particulars of the various lots to be offered for competition, and now on view. As the privilege of viewing in this instance was confined to those who possessed tickets, I did not apply for one, as I knew that the wish would be attributed to curiosity, and possibly a worse construction be put upon it, through my being a stranger in the place.

Passing onwards through the assembled throng, I got into a more secluded part of the city, and came upon a large burial-ground, in which many of the monuments erected to the memory of the dead were of a very expensive description. One in particular attracted my notice; this, on inquiry of a gentlemanly-looking man, who, like myself, was inclined to "meditate among the tombs," I ascertained had been erected by the relatives of a planter, who had resided in an adjoining state, but who had several cotton plantations within ten miles of Charleston; these he occasionally visited, but in general confided to the care of an overseer, who lived with his family on one of them. The season anterior to his last visit had been a very unpropitious one, and he was much dissatisfied with the management. To prevent a recurrence of this loss, and, under the strong impression that the hands were not worked as they should be, he resolved to inspect the plantations himself, and administer some wholesome discipline in *propria persona;* for this purpose, he visited one of the plantations, intending afterwards to proceed to the others in rotation. It so happened that he arrived when not expected; and, finding his overseer absent, and many of the hands not as closely engaged as he wished, he became violently enraged. Summoning the overseer, he ordered all hands in front of the house to witness a punishment, and causing eight or ten of those whom he pointed out to be tied up at once and well whipped, stood by the while in uncontrollable anger to give directions. In the midst of the scene, and while urging greater severity, he was seized with a fit of apoplexy, which was of such a nature, that it at once closed his career, and he died instantaneously. Directly the man fell, the negroes collected round him and uttered cries and lamentations, and the poor wretch who was at the moment the victim of his brutality, on being untied, which was immediately done, joined in it. Notwithstanding that my companion had a decided leaning towards the extinction of slavery, (although he started various objections to its abolition,) I was quite inclined to believe his relation, having, when in Florida, met with a somewhat similar instance of the devotedness of the negro race, in an old woman who was bitterly bewailing the loss of her deceased mistress. The latter was an English lady, but not over kind to her, and reflected no credit on her countrywomen. The poor creature in touching strains enlarged upon her beauty and accomplishments, but when I questioned her as to her treatment of the negroes in general belonging to the estates, would say little on the subject, and shook her head; in it was plain that, like most females living in the south, she was a pampered worldling, entirely engrossed by principles of self-interest, and little regarding the welfare of her dependents, if not, as I have before observed, very severe towards them. She died prematurely, from the effects of one of those virulent fevers, that in southern latitudes are so often fatal to the inhabitants, especially to those who have been nurtured in Europe. Her encoffined remains were shipped on board a vessel, to be conveyed to England for burial, in accordance with her expressed wish. When the poor creature came to that part of her piteous tale, when, as she called her, her "beautiful angel of a mistress" was put in the coffin, and the estate hands were called in to take a last view of her (a custom in vogue there sometimes), she was overpowered with grief, and her utterance was so choked, that she could scarcely proceed.

During my stay in Charleston, I became acquainted with a gentleman of colour, who followed a lucrative business as a dealer of some kind, and who had formerly been a slave. The introduction arose in rather a singular way, it being through a proposition made to open a school for the education of coloured children, in which I took an interest.

Great opposition was offered to the scheme by the white rulers of the place, who declared the project illegal, the enactments passed subsequent and prior to the insurrection stringently forbidding it, or any attempt to impart secular knowledge to the slaves. Notwithstanding the violent threats used to prevent it, a meeting was however convened to be held at the house of the gentleman referred to, and which I resolved, though not unaccompanied with danger to my person, to take an active part in. I accordingly went to his home on the evening appointed; this was a spacious house, furnished in sumptuous style, with extensive premises adjoining, contiguous to the north end of the levee. I noticed that the walls were hung with good oil paintings gorgeously framed, principally family portraits, but the most prominent in position was that of the unfortunate Haytian chief, Toussaint L'Ouverture, whose cruel end, at the instigation of the vindictive Bonaparte, will for ever reflect shame on the French name as long as a sense of justice and love of virtue and probity exists in the bosom of mankind. Far be it from me to trample on the name of one whom retributive justice has consigned to the dust, but the cruelty of Napoleon towards this magnanimous prince, and his final barbarity in consigning him to a damp dungeon in a fastness amongst the Alps, where he perished in exile from his subjects and family after ten months' miserable endurance of the hardships wrongfully imposed on him, almost causes a feeling of exultation at the downfall of a despot, who, aiming at the sovereignty of the world, scrupled not to sacrifice virtue and good faith at the shrine of ambition. The fate of both chiefs was similar, for both perished in captivity--the one the victim, perhaps, of inordinate ambition, the other of unscrupulous avarice and envious malignity. The misfortunes of Toussaint L'Ouverture have indeed with justice been pronounced the "history of the negro race," for, in almost every instance where coloured men have pushed themselves above the common level, they have incurred the envy of white men, and, in too many instances, have been crushed by their overbearing tyranny.

The meeting was conducted with religious decorum, most, if not all, of the coloured gentlemen present being members of the Wesleyan connection. I was pleased with the temperate spirit in which their wrongs were discussed; and, after drawing up the rules, forming a committee, and arranging other necessary preliminaries, the meeting broke up.

On reaching my hotel on my return, I was at once waited upon by the landlord, who, in certainly a respectful manner, informed me that the interest I had the day before incautiously expressed regarding the school, had led to my being watched to the house where the meeting was held; and that, to avoid the unpleasantness which would result from my continuing to take any steps in the matter, and which might ensue, he said, from the suspicions excited, he strongly advised that I should the next day address a letter to the editor of the principal newspaper in the city, repudiating all connection with a movement calculated, he said, to disturb the public mind, and, perhaps, cause disturbance. This I refused to do, but told him I did not intend to figure prominently in the matter, and that my stay in the city would be very limited. He then related several instances of mob law, which had been enacted-within the twelve months preceding, which, he said, were quite necessary to maintain southern rights, and which he did not fail to let me know he fully concurred in. After this hint, conveyed, I must say, in a friendly spirit, whatever my private opinion was as to the occasion of it, I mingled, during the remainder of my stay, very little with the frequenters of his establishment--a policy which I considered necessary from personal considerations; and, owing to this cautious behaviour, I was not afterwards interfered with, though often eyed with suspicion.

The school was opened during my stay, but continued so but a short time, the virulent conduct of the constables, supported by some of the citizens and the civil authorities, compelling its discontinuance. This is not to be wondered at, when it is remembered that the old statute law of South Carolina prohibits the education of negroes, bond or free, under a penalty of fine and imprisonment; and, although before the recent *emeute* it was falling into disuse, that event revived its enforcement with ancient malignity.

The free negro gentleman, at whose house the preliminaries for opening the school referred to were gone through, informed me, on a subsequent occasion, that the constant vexations and annoyances he was subjected to, owing to the prejudice in the minds of southern people regarding colour, would compel him to relinquish his business, and proceed either to Canada or to the free states. He deplored the alternative much, as he had been born and bred a slave in Carolina, and, by untiring assiduity, had saved money enough to emancipate himself and his wife; "In fact," he added, "I feel this is my country, and leaving it will come hard." He had a numerous family, which he maintained in great respectability, and his business being a profitable one made him more reluctant to abandon it and the advantages that otherwise would attend his continuance in Charleston. He hospitably entertained me at his home, and appeared highly gratified at meeting with a white man who felt disposed to regard him with equality.

After dining at his house one day, he took me a ride round the suburbs of the city, which I noticed were flat and exceedingly uninteresting. We returned by way of the Marine Parade, which is certainly a *chef d'oeuvre* of its kind. This is on the south side of the city, and commands a magnificent sea-view. It is raised far above the sea, and laid out with carriage-drives and paths for pedestrians. Far out, looking towards Cape Hatteras, is a fort on an island; this is always garrisoned by a detachment of U.S. troops, and of late years has been used as a receptacle for those daring chiefs among the Indians, who, by their indomitable courage, have been the terror of the United States frontier. Here that hero Oceola, chief of the Seminoles, died not long before, in captivity, from excessive grief, caused by the treachery of certain American officers, who, under a pretended truce, seized him and his attendant warriors. Below us in the bay we could see the fins of several sharks, ploughing the waves in search of prey; while the constant sailing to and fro of Cuba fruit-boats, laden with bananas, pawpaws, pine-apples, and every luxury that and contiguous islands afford, enlivened the scene, which altogether was one of extraordinary beauty.

There was a large assemblage of ladies and gentlemen promenading, and, as I rode with my friend, I had some very furtive glances from the crowd, which were intended, no doubt, to remind me that my keeping such company was *infra dig.*, if not open to suspicion. There was in truth no little hazard in riding about in public with a man against whose acquaintance I had a short time before been cautioned, and I felt my position rather an uncomfortable one.

Had some of the young blood of Charleston been up, there is little doubt but that I must have left the place *sans ceremonie.* Possessed of a natural urbanity, or, what in elevated society amongst white people, would be termed true politeness, the manner of the well-bred negro is prepossessing. This was very remarkable in my coloured friend, who was well informed, and possessed a refinement and intelligence I had never before met with in any of his race. On the subject of enslavement he would at first venture few observations, confining himself to those inconveniences and annoyances that affected him individually; he, however, became, after a time, more communicative.

On the whole, at first, I was not a little apprehensive that my coloured acquaintance was under the impression that my friendship was not sincere, although he did not say as much in his conversation; the impression, however, soon left me, after a further intimacy. I considered then, and do now, that the suspicion was quite excusable, the Jesuitical practices and underhand trickery descended to by the white population in the slave states, in order to ascertain how individuals stand affected, are so numerous, that the coloured people are obliged to be wary of those they either suspect, or of whom, being strangers, they know little.

I remember well, whilst riding with him on the occasion I have already referred to, we drove past a white man on horseback, who (as is common in Charleston), was correcting his negro in the street. The poor fellow was writhing under the cruel infliction of a flagellation with a raw-hide, and rent the air with his cries. This only increased the rage of his master, who seemed to take delight in striking his face and ears. I eagerly watched the scene, and, as we passed, leaned over the back of the gig. My companion, fearing, I suppose, lest the sight might provoke in me some exclamation, and thus get us into notice, nudged me violently with his elbow, saying at the same time, hurriedly, "Don't heed, don't heed." My blood was getting hot, and but for my companion, my passion would, in all probability, have got the better of my discretion, and I should without remedy have been involved in a dispute, if not immediately apprehended. As we rode on, I adverted to this barefaced exhibition of tyranny in an open thoroughfare, which, I remarked, was sufficient proof of the iniquity of the system, in spite of the assertions made by the southerners to the contrary. In reply to this, all my companion remarked was, "Did you never see that done before?" My answer was, I had seen negroes cruelly treated on estates, and elsewhere, but that this scene was the more revolting from its being enacted in the open highway. Seeing that he was anxious to avoid the subject, and that the observations he had made were drawn from him by my remarks, I remained silent, and, wrapped in deep reflections on the outrage we had witnessed, at length reached his dwelling. The occurrence I suppose somewhat affected my spirits, for soon after we got into the drawing-room, no one else being present, my friend addressed me, no doubt observing my depression, nearly as follows. "Sir, you seem to have a tender compassion for my poor countrymen; would to God white men were all as feeling here. The system is an accursed one, but what can we do but bear it patiently? Every hand seems against us, and we dare not speak for ourselves." I told him I deeply sympathised with his oppressed countrymen, and lived in hope that before long the public mind in America would be aroused from its apathy, and the accumulated wrongs of the race be redressed. His only reply was, "God grant it, I hope so too."

In Charleston there exist several charitable institutions, but these, I believe, with only one exception, are for the benefit of poor white people. The innate benevolence of the human heart is thus, in the midst of dire oppression, wont to hold its sway, notwithstanding the poisonous influences that surround. But the pro-slavery business neutralizes these would-be benefactors, and taints all their endeavours, under the cloak of benevolence, to remove the odium it so justly incurs. "Liberate your slaves, and then I will talk to you about religion and charity," were the emphatic words of an eminent northern divine in his correspondence with the committee of a benevolent institution in the south, some years ago, and the admonition speaks as forcibly now as it did then.

As you walk the streets of Charleston, rows of greedy vultures, with sapient look, sit on the parapets of the houses, watching for offal. These birds are great blessings in warm climates, and in Carolina a fine of ten dollars is inflicted for wantonly destroying them. They appeared to be quite conscious of their privileges, and sailed down from the house-tops into the streets, where they stalked about, hardly caring to move out of the way of the horses and carriages passing. They were of an eagle-brown colour, and many of them appeared well conditioned, even to obesity. At night scores of dogs collect in the streets, and yelp and bark in the most annoying manner. This it is customary to remedy by a gun being fired from a window at the midnight interlopers, when they disperse in great terror. I should remark that this is a common nuisance in warm latitudes. Some of these animals live in the wilds, and, like jackals, steal into the towns at night to eke out a scanty subsistence. At first my rest was greatly disturbed by their noisy yelpings, but I soon became accustomed to the inconvenience, and thought little of it.

The warmth of the climate induces great lassitude and indisposition to exertion, *alias* indolence. I began to experience this soon after arriving in the south. This, which in England would be called laziness, is encouraged by the most trifling offices being performed by slaves. The females in particular give way to this inertness, and active women are seldom to be met with, the wives of men in affluent circumstances being in general like pampered children, and suffering dreadfully from *ennui*. On one occasion an English gentleman at Charleston, with whom I became acquainted, and whose hospitality I shall never forget, when conversing on the subject, addressed me thus: "Good, active wives are seldom to be met with in this state, amongst the natives; I may say, hardly ever; the females are nurtured in indolence, and in seeking what they term a settlement, look more to the man's means than the likelihood of living happily with him. There is no disguising it--the considera--with them is a ***sine qua non***. Few girls would refuse a man who possessed a goodly number of slaves, though they were sure his affections would be shared by some of the best-looking of the females amongst them, and his conduct towards the remainder that of a very demon." These sentiments I very soon ascertained to be in no way libellous. A southern wife, if she is prodigally furnished with dollars to "go shopping," apparently considers it no drawback to her happiness if some brilliant mulatto or quadroon woman ensnares her husband. Of course there are exceptions, but the patriarchal usage is so engrafted in society there, that it elicits little notice or comment. Nor, from what I gleaned, are the ladies themselves immaculate, as may be inferred from the occasional quadroon aspect of their progeny.

The Jews are a very numerous and influential body in Charleston, and monopolize many of its corporate honours. They were described as very haughty and captious; this, however, is saying no more of the stock of Israel than is observable all over the world, hen they are in prosperous circumstances, although, when this is not the case, perhaps none of the human family are so abject and servile, not excepting slaves themselves. In process of time, these people bid fair to concentrate in themselves most of the wealth and influence of Charleston. If their perseverance (which is here indomitable) should attain this result, they will be in pretty much the same position there that Pharaoh occupied over their race in Egypt in olden time, and, if reports speak true, will wield the sceptre of authority over their captives in a somewhat similar style. Avarice is the besetting sin of the Israelite, and here his slaves are taxed beyond endurance. To exact the utmost from his labour is the constant aim, and I was informed that many of the slaves belonging to Jews were sent out, and compelled on the Saturday night to bring in a much larger sum than it was reasonably possible the poor creatures could earn, and if not successful, they were subjected to the most cruel treatment.

Not long after my arrival in Charleston, I several times met a young coloured man, who was of so prepossessing an appearance, that I felt desirous to become acquainted with him, and, as I was at a loss to find my way to the residence of the mayor, a good opportunity one day offered, and I addressed him. He very courteously took me to the street in which the house was situated, and we talked on general topics as we went--in the course of which he stated, he was saving money for his ransom, and in two years intended to proceed to Montreal, in Canada. I could see, however, that the free manner in which we conversed attracted the attention of three or four individuals as we passed them--these would stop as if to satisfy their curiosity, some even took the trouble to watch us out of sight; looking back, I several times saw one more impertinent-looking than some others eyeing us intently, and once I fancied I saw him turn as if to overtake us. This curiosity I had often perceived before, but, as disagreeable results might follow, I invariably made a practice to take no notice of it when in the company of a coloured individual. A smile played upon the features of my dusky companion, as I turned to observe the inquisitive fellows I have referred to; perhaps I was taken for a negro-stealer, but, as I treated my companion with equality, I was most likely set down as one of those dangerous personages, who, through zeal in the cause of emancipation, sometimes penetrate, into the slave districts, and are accused (with what degree of justice I cannot tell) of infusing into the minds of the slaves discontented notions and agrarian principles.

As I met, on the occasion I have just referred to, an individual who knew I had felt an interest in endeavouring to establish the school for the education of negro children, the result of which I have already mentioned, I was apprehensive that the *contretemps* would have exposed me to the unpleasantness of at least being shunned afterwards as a man entertaining principles inimical to southern interests--and, however resolute I felt to pursue an independent course while I remained in Charleston, I could not shake off a fear I vaguely entertained of a public recognition by a deeply prejudiced and ignorant populace, who, once set on, do not hesitate to proceed to disagreeable extremes. This fear was enhanced in no little degree by the operation I had witnessed, of the tarring and feathering process practised by enraged citizens in the Missouri country, which I have before described.

The most degrading phrase that can be applied in the south to those white individuals who sympathize in the wrongs inflicted on the African race, I soon found to be, that "he associates with niggers." Thus a kind-hearted individual at once "loses caste" among his fellow citizens and, invidious though it certainly is, many slave-owners are deterred by this consideration, blended with a politic regard for their own safety, from exercising that benevolence towards their dependents which they sincerely feel; placed, as it were, under a sort of social ban, such men artfully conceal their sentiments from the public, and, by a more lenient treatment of their own hands, quiet their consciences; while, at the same time, they blunt their sense of what is honest, upright, just, and manly. Instances have occasionally occurred where men of correct principles have so far succumbed to this sense of duty, as to liberate their slaves. These are, however, rare occurrences, and, when they do happen, are usually confined to men of sterling religious principles, who, like that great exception, the respectable class of people called Quakers, in America, refuse, from a conviction of the enormity of the evil, to recognize as members those who hold or traffic in slaves.

It is through the influence of such men that the iniquities of the system become exposed to public view, and remedies are sometimes, in flagrant cases of cruelty, applied. The legislatures of the several slave states, however, have given such absolute dominion, by a rigorous code of laws, to the owner, that the greatest enormities may be committed almost with impunity, or at least with but a remote chance of justice having its legitimate sway.

The mass of slave-owners are interested in concealing enormities committed by their fellows, and are backed by a venal press, which, whether bribed or not (and there is every reason to suspect that this is often the case), puts such a construction on *outrage*, by garbled *reports*, as to turn the tide of sympathy from the victim to the perpetrator. No editor, possessing the least leaven of anti-slavery principles, would be patronized; and it not infrequently happens that such men are mobbed and driven perforce to leave the slave, for the more northern or free, states. Here they stand a better chance, but, in many instances, the prejudice, it is said, follows their course, and southern influence occasions their bankruptcy or non-success.

The practice, so common in the slave states, of the citizens congregating at the bars of hotels or cafes in the towns and cities to while away the time, renders attendance at such places the readiest means of ascertaining the state of the public mind on any engrossing subject, opinions being here freely discussed, not, however, without bias and anger; on the contrary, the practice is most sectarian, and frequently involves deadly feuds and personal encounters, these latter being of everyday occurrence. Ever since I had been in the southern states, my attention had been attracted to the swarms of well-dressed loungers at cafes and hotels. At first, like many other travellers, I was deluded by the notion that these idlers were men of independent means, but my mind was soon disabused of this fallacy. I ascertained that the greater portion of these belong to that numerous class in America known as sporting gentlemen; in plainer terms, gamblers. Some of these men had belonged to the higher walks of life; these were the more "retiring few" who (probably through a sense of shame not quite extinguished) felt rather disposed to shrink from than to attract attention. The majority of these idlers were impudent-looking braggarts, who, with jaunty air and coxcombical show of superiority, endeavoured to enforce their own opinions, and to silence those of every one else.

There was also another class of frequenters at such places; this consisted of tradesmen who pass much of their time hanging about at such resorts, to the great detriment of their individual affairs; and, lastly, such travellers as might be stopping in the town, who, through *ennui* and inveterate habit, had left their hotels, and sauntered "up town" (as they call gadding about), to hear the news of the day.

Soon ascertaining that such places were the best, and, excepting the public prints, the only resort to ascertain the latest intelligence, and to collect information respecting the movements of the black population, and the company, however exceptionable, being termed there respectable, I adopted the plan, on several successive evenings, of quietly smoking a cigar and listening to passing observations and remarks. Some of these were disgusting enough; so much so, that I will not offend my readers by repeating them. Suffice it to say, that any individual possessing the slightest pretensions to the name of gentleman, in any hotel I had visited in England, on indulging in the indecorous language I heard at these places, would, by a very summary process, have met with ejectment, without ceremony. Here, however, a laxity of moral feeling prevails, that stifles all sense of propriety; and scurrility, obscene language, and filthy jests, of which the coloured population are, I suppose, per force of habit, the principal butts, form the chief attractions of such places of resort to their vitiated frequenters.

In the course of these visits I was present at some angry altercations; one of these referred to the recent visit of an individual who was termed by the disputants an "incendiary abolitionist," and who, it appeared, had been detected in the act of distributing tracts, which had been published at Salem, in Massachusetts, exposing the disabilities the African race were labouring under. Extracts from one of these tracts were read, and appeared very much to increase the violence of the contending parties, one of whom insisted that the publication contained nothing but what might be read by every slave in the sacred Scriptures, and that, therefore, it could not be classed as dangerous, although he admitted that it contained notions of "human rights" that were calculated to imbue the mind of the "niggers" with unbecoming ideas. These sentiments did not at all accord with those of the company, and several expressions of doubt as to the soundness of the speaker's own pro-slavery principles, together with the increasing excitement, caused him to withdraw from the contest. His immediate antagonist, who was evidently the leading man on the occasion, enlarged on the danger attending the sufferance of such men at large in the slave states, and proceeded, with great volubility, to quote various passages from the Black Code to show that the Legislature had contemplated the intrusion of such pestilent fellows, and had, in fact, given full power to remedy the evil, if the citizens chose to exercise it; and went on to observe, that the rights of southern people were now-a-days invaded on every hand, and it behoved them to stand in their own defence, his advice, he said, was, if the municipal authorities let the fellow go, to form a committee of justice to adjudicate on the case, and if it was considered conducive to the public weal, to administer salutary punishment. This proposal was uproariously applauded, and four of the citizens present, with the last speaker for chairman, were named on the spot to watch the case. "And now," added this gentleman, "we'll have a gin sling round for success." I heard the day following that the individual who was the subject of the foregoing proceedings, was accused before the mayor, who dismissed the case with a caution, advising him to leave the city with all dispatch, to avoid disagreeable consequences. This the man, by the aid of a constable, managed to do, that functionary, no doubt for a consideration, taking him to the city prison, and locking him up until nightfall, when he was assisted to leave the place, disguised as a soldier. This, I was informed by a friend, to whom I afterwards related it, was one of those commotions that occur almost daily in southern towns and cities.

Such lawless frequenters of hotels, taverns, and cafes, form a kind of social police, and scarcely a stranger visits the place without his motives for the visit being canvassed, and his business often exposed, much to his great annoyance and inconvenience.

So accustomed do American travellers in the south appear, to this system of internal surveillance, that I several times noticed strangers at the hotel or cafe counters openly explaining the object of their visits, and if there is nothing to conceal, however annoying the alternative appears, I am convinced the policy is not had, a host of suspicions being silenced by such a course.

In my travels on the whole route from New York to Charleston, I discovered a most unjustifiable and impertinent disposition to pry into the business of others. If I was questioned once, I am sure I was at least fifty times, by my fellow--travellers from time to time as to my motive for visiting America, and my intended proceedings. I found, however', that a certain reserve was an efficient remedy. Captain Waterton, of South American celebrity, as an ornithologist, and who visited North America in his travels, mentions that if you confide your affairs and intentions when questioned, the Americans reciprocate that confidence by relating their own. My own experience, however, did not corroborate this view of the case, for, though loquacious in the extreme, and gifted, so that to use a Yankee phrase, they would "talk a dog's hind-leg off," they are in general cautious not to divulge their secrets. To say the least of it, the habit of prying into the business of others, is one totally unbecoming a well-ordered state of society, which the American, speaking generally, is decidedly not. It is extremely annoying, from the unpleasant feeling it excites, that you are suspected if not watched (this applies forcibly to the slave districts); and it is a habit that has arisen purely from the incongruity of society at large on the American continent, and a want of that subdivision of class that exists in Europe.

During my visits to the various hotels while I remained in Charleston, for the purpose of collecting information, I was several times interrogated in a barefaced manner by the visitors who frequent those places, as to my politics, and especially as to my principles in regard to the institution of slavery; now, as I was not unaware that my intimacy with the gentleman of colour, which I have already referred to, had got abroad, I was obliged to be extremely guarded in my replies on such occasions. It was on one of these that I felt myself in great hazard, for two individuals in the company were discussing with much energy, the question of amalgamation (that is, marriage, contracted between black and white men and women), and I was listening intently to their altercation, when suddenly one of them, eyeing me with malicious gaze, no doubt having noticed my attention to the colloquy, said,

"Your opinion, stranger, on this subject; I guess you understand it torrably well, as you seem to be pretty hard on B----'s eldest daughter." This unexpected sally rather alarmed me, for the name he mentioned was that of my coloured friend I have before alluded to, and whose daughter I had only met once, and that at her father's house.

I scarcely knew what to reply, but thought it best to put on a bold face, so facing the man, I thanked him with much irony for the inuendo, and said, it was a piece of impudence I thought very much like him from what I had overheard.

This was said in a resolute tone, and the fellow quailed before it, his reply being, "Now stranger, don't get angry, I saw you the other day at B----'s house, and could not tell what to make of it, but I hope you don't think that I was in arnest."

I replied to this, that I knew best what business I had at B----'s house, and that his plan was to mind his own business. I then left him, apparently highly indignant, but in fact glad to make my escape. Like bullies all the world over, the southern ones are cowards; there is, however, great danger here in embroiling yourself with such characters, the pistol and bowie knife being instantly resorted to if the quarrel becomes serious. I saw this braggart on several occasions afterwards, but he evidently kept aloof, and was disinclined to venture in the part of the room I occupied. I ascertained that he kept a dry goods store in King-street, and was a boisterous fellow, often involved in quarrels.

The discussion on amalgamation, which is a very vexed one, was again introduced on a subsequent occasion; a planter from the north of the state having (as is sometimes the case) sold off everything he possessed, and removed to the State of Maine, taking with him a young quadroon woman, with the intention of making her his lawful wife, and living there retired. After the expression of a variety of opinions as to what this man deserved, some being of opinion that the subject ought to be mooted in the legislature at Washington--others, that his whole effects ought to be escheated, for the benefit of the public treasury--and by far the greater number that he ought to be summarily dealt with at the hands of the so-considered outraged citizens, which, in other language, meant "lynched,"--it was stated, by a very loquacious Yankee-looking fellow present, who made himself prominent in the discussion, that it was the opinion of the company, that any man marrying a woman with negro blood in her veins, should be hanged, as a traitor to southern interests and a bad citizen. This sentiment was loudly applauded, and, had the unfortunate subject of it been in Charleston or near it, he would, in all probability, have been called to account. To me it appeared remarkable, that men, who are always boasting of the well-ordered institutions of their country (slavery being a very important one, be it remembered), should be ever ready to set aside all law, and, as it were, by ***ex parte*** evidence alone, inflict summary vengeance on the offender; I was, however, always of opinion, when amongst them, that four-fifths of the men would rejoice if all law were abrogated, and the passions of the people allowed to govern the country, thus constituting themselves judges in their own case, and trampling under foot every semblance of justice, equity, and common propriety. As it is, in many parts of the Union, the judges and magistrates are notoriously awed by the people, and the most perfidious wretches are suffered to escape the hands of justice. A full confirmation of this is to be found in the frequent outrages against law and order reported in the newspapers, and which there elicit little regard.

Walking for a stroll, a day or two after, in the vicinity of the Marine-promenade, I saw a strange-looking cavalcade approaching. Two armed overseers were escorting five negroes, recently captured, to the city gaol. The poor creatures were so heavily shackled, that they could walk but slowly, and their brutal conductors kept urging them on, chiefly by coarse language and oaths, now and then accompanied by a severe stroke with a slave-whip carried by one of them. The recovered fugitives looked very dejected, and were, no doubt, brooding over the consequences of their conduct. The elder of the party, a stout fellow of about forty-five years old, of very sullen look, had a distinct brand on his forehead of the initials S.T.R. I afterwards inquired what these brand-marks signified, supposing, naturally, that they were the initials of the name of his present or former owner. My informant, who was a by-stander, stated that he was, no doubt, an incorrigibly bad fellow, and that the initials S.T.R. were often used in such cases. I inquired their signification, when, to my astonishment, he replied it might be, "Stop the rascal," and added that private signals were in constant use among the inland planters, as he called them, who, he said, suffered so much by their hands running away, that it was absolutely necessary to adopt a plan of the kind for security. He further stated, that such incorrigibles, when caught, were never allowed to leave the plantations, so that if they ventured abroad, they carried the warrant for their immediate arrest with them. "But," he went on, "people are beginning to dislike such severity, and a new code of regulations, backed by the Legislature, is much talked of by the innovators, as we call them, to prevent such practices." I have no doubt this man owned slaves himself.

I said I thought myself that the policy of kindness would answer better than such severities, and it would be well if slave-holders generally were to try it.

"Ah, stranger," he replied, "I see you don't understand things here, down south. Don't you know that people who are over kind get imposed on? This is specially the case with slaves; treat them well, and you'll soon find them running off, or complaining. The only way to manage niggers is to keep them down, then you can control them, but not else."

It has been urged a thousand times in defence of the upholders of slavery in its various ramifications, that they are in reality, as a body, opposed to the system, and would readily conform to any change that would be sufficiently comprehensive to indemnify them from present and future loss. From conversations heard in South Carolina, and other slave districts, I am quite satisfied that this is a misrepresentation, and that the generality of proprietors regard any change as a dangerous innovation, and that, far from reluctantly following the occupation of traders in flesh and blood, it is quite congenial to the vitiated tastes of the greater portion of southern citizens, whose perverted notions of justice and propriety are clamorously expressed on the most trivial occasions. In whatever sphere of society amongst them you go, you find the subject of "protecting their rights" urged with impetuosity; the same rancorous feeling towards men of abolitionist sentiments, and the same deprecation of the slave race. To decry the negroes in public opinion is one of their constant rules of action, and if an individual attempts to assert their equal rights with mankind at large, he is considered as disaffected towards southern interests, and, if not openly threatened, as I have before observed in this work, is unceremoniously talked down.' It is thus often dangerous to broach the subject, and if an individual, more daring than people generally are when in the plague-infected latitudes of slavery, attempts to repudiate the views so unhesitatingly expressed by the pro-slavery advocates, that the negro race is but the connecting link between man and the brute creation, he is looked upon with disgust, and his society contemned. This overbearing conduct is so ingrained, that it shows itself on the most trifling occasions, in their intercourse with their fellow-citizens.

Argumentative facts might be produced ***ad infinitum*** to prove that the legal enactments for the government of the slave states of America have been framed so as to vest in the proprietor as much control over the lives and persons of those they hold in servitude as any animal in the category of plantation stock. This in my tour through that region of moral darkness and despair, the state of Louisiana, I had numberless opportunities of observing, which would not fail to convince the most sceptical; and if I have passed over many of these in the foregoing pages, it is because the incidents themselves (though proving that the slightest approach to independent action, or opposition to the depraved wills of their tyrannical superiors, is at once visited with consequences that make me shudder to reflect upon) were of too trivial a nature to interest the general reader. I will, however, copy here an extract from a paper published in Virginia, the *Richmond Times* for August, 1852, which must, I think, tend to remove any doubts, if they exist in the mind of the reader, that the conclusions I have come to from personal observation are correct, and sufficient to prove that the despotic Nicholas of Russia himself does not exercise more absolute control over the lives and liberties of the degraded serfs he rules, than the slave-appropriators of America do over their victims.

The newspaper in question is a highly popular one with the aristocratical slave-owners of Virginia, and the editor one of those champions of the unjust and iniquitous system who invariably meet with extensive patronage in every part of the southern states.

"A FIELD-HAND SHOT.--A gentleman named Ball, overseer to Mr. Edward T. Taylor, finding it necessary to chastise a field-hand, attempted to do so in the field. The negro resisted, and made fight, and, being the stronger of the two, gave the overseer a beating, and then betook himself to the woods. Mr. Ball, as soon as he could do so, mounted his horse, and, proceeding to Mr. Taylor's residence, informed him of what had occurred. Taylor, in company with Ball, repaired to the corn-field, to which the negro had returned, and demanded to know the cause of his conduct. The negro replied that Ball attempted to flog him, and he would not submit to it. Taylor said he should, and ordered him to cross his hands, at the same time directing Ball to seize him. Ball did so, but perceiving the negro had attempted to draw a knife, told Mr. Taylor of it, who immediately sprang from his horse, and, drawing a pistol, shot the negro dead at his feet."

The *Richmond Reporter*, a contemporary of the *Times*, commented on this impious affair as follows:--"Mr. Taylor did what every man who has the management of negroes ought to do; enforce obedience, or kill them."

It is the practice of the inhabitants of Charleston, in common, I believe, with all owners of slaves in towns or cities in the slave states, who have not employment sufficient for them at home, or when the slave is a cripple, to send them out to seek their own maintenance. In such cases the slave is compelled to give an account of what he has earned during the week, at his owner's house, where he attends on Saturday evenings for the purpose. A fixed sum is generally demanded, in proportion to the average value of such labour at the time. I was informed that it frequently happens, that the master exacts the utmost the slave can earn, so that the miserable pittance left is scarcely sufficient to sustain nature; this, no doubt, accounts for the haggard, care-worn appearance of such labourers, for, with few exceptions, I found hands thus sent out, more miserably clad and less hale than the common run of slaves. On the other hand, if a slave is a good handicraftsman, he is able to earn more than his master demands; such instances are, however, rare. These are the men who, by dint of hard work and thrifty habits, accumulate sufficient eventually to obtain manumission. There is, in most cases, a strict eye kept on such hands, and if the boon is attained, it is in general by stealthy means.

At my boarding-house in Charleston, I often saw negro laundresses who called for linen; one of these in particular, I noticed, seemed to be in habitual low spirits; on one occasion she appeared to be in unusual distress, in consequence of one of the boarders leaving the house in her debt. She said that her owner would certainly punish her if she did not make up the required sum, and where to procure it she could not tell. I was touched by her tale, and immediately opened a subscription amongst the boarders in the house, and succeeded in collecting a trifle over the amount she had lost; this I handed her, and she went on her way rejoicing.

I was told by a Carolinian who lodged at this house, that the practice of sending out slaves to earn money in the way I have described, has been in vogue from time immemorial, and that it was such a profitable mode of realizing by slave labour, that it was followed more extensively in that state now than formerly.

I will conclude this part of my narration, by quoting the words of a powerful writer on the subject of slavery as I have witnessed its operation in America.

"Amongst the afflicting ills which the wickedness of man has established upon earth, the greatest beyond compare is slavery. Indeed, its consequences are so dreadful, the sins which it engenders are of such gigantic proportions, and all its accompaniments are so loathsome and hideous, that the minds of benevolent persons revolt from contemplating it, as offering a spectacle of crime and cruelty, too deep for a remedy, and too vast for sympathy. Slavery is an infinite evil, the calculations of its murders, its rapine, its barbarities, its deeds of lust and licentiousness, though authenticated by the most unquestionable authorities, would produce a total of horrors too great to be believed; and to narrate the history of these cruelties which have been perpetrated by American slave-masters within the last five years alone, would be to tell idle fables in the opinions of those who have not deeply studied the tragical subject. If we take the United States of America, where the outcry against slavery is greater than in any other country under heaven, and where we hear more of religion and revivalism, more of bustle and machinery of piety, a country setting itself up as a beacon of freedom; then does slavery amongst such a people appear transcendently wicked; a sin, which, in addition to its usual cruelty and selfishness, is in them loaded with hypocrisy and ingratitude. With hypocrisy, as it relates to their pretensions to liberty, and with ingratitude, as it relates to that God who gave them to be free. This, indeed, makes all the institutions of America, civil and religious, little better than a solemn mockery, a tragical jest for the passers-by of other nations, who, seeing two millions and a half of slaves held in fetters by vaunting freemen and ostentatious patriots, wag the head at the disgusting sight, and cry out deridingly to degraded America, 'The worm is spread under thee, and the worms cover thee.'"

My original intention of settling in America having been frustrated by ill health and other causes, I embarked on board a fine barque bound for Liverpool, where, after a favourable run of three weeks, we arrived in safety. Nothing worth noting occurred on the passage, except a fracas between the captain and the first mate, whom the former had discovered to be ignorant of the art of navigation, and who had, it appeared, been engaged in a hurry on the eve of the vessel's departure from Charleston.

One day, comparing the result of a solar observation with the mate, and finding him out in his calculations, the captain accused him, in great anger, of imposition, in offering his services as an efficient person to navigate the ship. On my endeavouring to pacify him, he turned to me, in a violent passion, and exclaimed, "This man, sir, is 400 miles out in his reckoning--and where would you and the ship be, do you think, if I were washed overboard!" this argument was too cogent to be combated, and so I interfered no more. He ordered the mate to go to the forecastle, and refused to admit him to the cabin during the remainder of the passage. The mate was much irritated at this treatment, and, after a violent altercation, one day rushed to his chest and brought up two pistols, one of which he presented in the face of the captain, daring him at the same time to utter another word. The captain, highly incensed, instantly descended the companion-way to the cabin, and shortly after appeared with a blunderbuss, which he proceeded to prime. I was in a terrible state of mind at this juncture, and fully expected a fearful tragedy; this, however, was averted by the interference of another passenger, who stood between the parties.

A violent storm overtook us in doubling Cape Hatteras soon after we sailed, which, besides damaging the bulwarks of the vessel, tore some of the sails to shivers; our ship stood it, however, gallantly, and, after that occurrence, we had favourable weather the remainder of the voyage.

I was awaked early in the morning of the twenty-first day we had been at sea, by a cry from the man at the helm, of "Great Ormes Head," and, hurrying on my clothes, I gained the deck. The high hills could be indistinctly seen through the morning haze, and the sight was accompanied with joyful feelings to all on board. This enthusiasm was even communicated to the captain himself, who, since the affair with the mate, had been very much disposed to be sullen and unfriendly.

I never could form a correct estimate of this man's character, but it was very evident he wished to pass for a pious man. He was a native of the eastern state of Massachusetts, and told me he had a family there. As to religion, I believe he had none, though he was a Methodist by profession. I could often hear him praying audibly in his state-room on board, with much apparent feeling--but so little did these devotional fits aid him in curbing his wicked temper, that, even when engaged in this manner, he would, if anything extraordinary occurred on deck to disturb him, rush up the companion-way, and rate and swear at the sailors awfully.

Soon after making Ormes Head, a pilot came on board, and, with a fair wind, we proceeded towards the river Mersey.

After my wanderings in the slave-stricken regions of the south, and my escapes in Florida, the sight of the hospitable shores of my native country did more, I think, to renovate my injured health, than all the drastics of the most eminent physicians in the world; certain it is, that, from this time, I gradually recovered, and, by the blessing of the Great Giver of all good, have been fully restored to that greatest of sublunary benefits--vigorous health; a consummation I at one time almost despaired of.

www.bookjungle.com *email: sales@bookjungle.com fax: 630-214-0564 mail: Book Jungle PO Box 2226 Champaign, IL 61825*

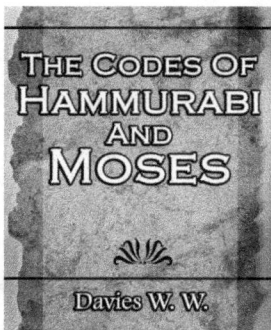

The Codes Of Hammurabi And Moses
W. W. Davies

QTY

The discovery of the Hammurabi Code is one of the greatest achievements of archaeology, and is of paramount interest, not only to the student of the Bible, but also to all those interested in ancient history...

Religion **ISBN:** *1-59462-338-4* **Pages:132**
MSRP $12.95

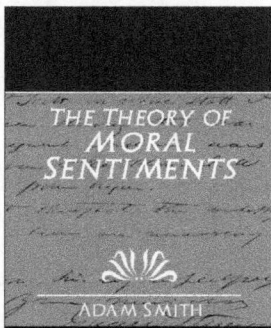

The Theory of Moral Sentiments
Adam Smith

QTY

This work from 1749. contains original theories of conscience amd moral judgment and it is the foundation for systemof morals.

Philosophy **ISBN:** *1-59462-777-0* **Pages:536**
MSRP $19.95

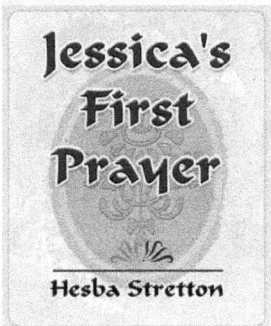

Jessica's First Prayer
Hesba Stretton

QTY

In a screened and secluded corner of one of the many railway-bridges which span the streets of London there could be seen a few years ago, from five o'clock every morning until half past eight, a tidily set-out coffee-stall, consisting of a trestle and board, upon which stood two large tin cans, with a small fire of charcoal burning under each so as to keep the coffee boiling during the early hours of the morning when the work-people were thronging into the city on their way to their daily toil...

Pages:84

Childrens **ISBN:** *1-59462-373-2* *MSRP $9.95*

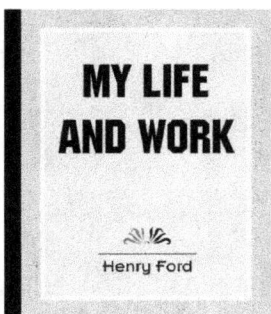

My Life and Work
Henry Ford

QTY

Henry Ford revolutionized the world with his implementation of mass production for the Model T automobile. Gain valuable business insight into his life and work with his own auto-biography... "We have only started on our development of our country we have not as yet, with all our talk of wonderful progress, done more than scratch the surface. The progress has been wonderful enough but..."

Pages:300

Biographies/ **ISBN:** *1-59462-198-5* *MSRP $21.95*

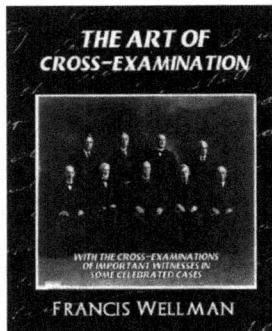

The Art of Cross-Examination
Francis Wellman

QTY

I presume it is the experience of every author, after his first book is published upon an important subject, to be almost overwhelmed with a wealth of ideas and illustrations which could readily have been included in his book, and which to his own mind, at least, seem to make a second edition inevitable. Such certainly was the case with me; and when the first edition had reached its sixth impression in five months, I rejoiced to learn that it seemed to my publishers that the book had met with a sufficiently favorable reception to justify a second and considerably enlarged edition. ..

Pages:412

Reference   ISBN: *1-59462-647-2*   *MSRP $19.95*

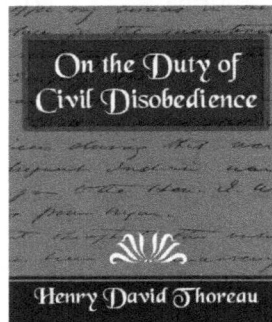

On the Duty of Civil Disobedience
Henry David Thoreau

QTY

Thoreau wrote his famous essay, On the Duty of Civil Disobedience, as a protest against an unjust but popular war and the immoral but popular institution of slave-owning. He did more than write—he declined to pay his taxes, and was hauled off to gaol in consequence. Who can say how much this refusal of his hastened the end of the war and of slavery ?

Law   ISBN: *1-59462-747-9*   **Pages:48**

MSRP $7.45

Dream Psychology Psychoanalysis for Beginners
Sigmund Freud

QTY

Sigmund Freud, born Sigismund Schlomo Freud (May 6, 1856 - September 23, 1939), was a Jewish-Austrian neurologist and psychiatrist who co-founded the psychoanalytic school of psychology. Freud is best known for his theories of the unconscious mind, especially involving the mechanism of repression; his redefinition of sexual desire as mobile and directed towards a wide variety of objects; and his therapeutic techniques, especially his understanding of transference in the therapeutic relationship and the presumed value of dreams as sources of insight into unconscious desires.

Pages:196

Psychology   ISBN: *1-59462-905-6*   *MSRP $15.45*

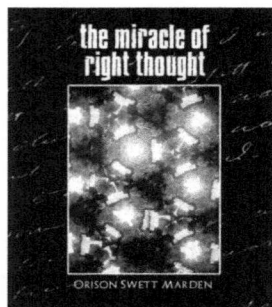

The Miracle of Right Thought
Orison Swett Marden

QTY

Believe with all of your heart that you will do what you were made to do. When the mind has once formed the habit of holding cheerful, happy, prosperous pictures, it will not be easy to form the opposite habit. It does not matter how improbable or how far away this realization may see, or how dark the prospects may be, if we visualize them as best we can, as vividly as possible, hold tenaciously to them and vigorously struggle to attain them, they will gradually become actualized, realized in the life. But a desire, a longing without endeavor, a yearning abandoned or held indifferently will vanish without realization.

Pages:360

Self Help   ISBN: *1-59462-644-8*   *MSRP $25.45*

QTY

☐ **The Rosicrucian Cosmo-Conception Mystic Christianity** *by Max Heindel* ISBN: *1-59462-188-8* **$38.95**
The Rosicrucian Cosmo-conception is not dogmatic, neither does it appeal to any other authority than the reason of the student. It is: not controversial, but is: sent forth in the, hope that it may help to clear... New Age/Religion Pages 646

☐ **Abandonment To Divine Providence** *by Jean-Pierre de Caussade* ISBN: *1-59462-228-0* **$25.95**
"The Rev. Jean Pierre de Caussade was one of the most remarkable spiritual writers of the Society of Jesus in France in the 18th Century. His death took place at Toulouse in 1751. His works have gone through many editions and have been republished... Inspirational/Religion Pages 400

☐ **Mental Chemistry** *by Charles Haanel* ISBN: *1-59462-192-6* **$23.95**
Mental Chemistry allows the change of material conditions by combining and appropriately utilizing the power of the mind. Much like applied chemistry creates something new and unique out of careful combinations of chemicals the mastery of mental chemistry... New Age Pages 354

☐ **The Letters of Robert Browning and Elizabeth Barret Barrett 1845-1846 vol II** ISBN: *1-59462-193-4* **$35.95**
by Robert Browning and Elizabeth Barrett Biographies Pages 596

☐ **Gleanings In Genesis (volume I)** *by Arthur W. Pink* ISBN: *1-59462-130-6* **$27.45**
Appropriately has Genesis been termed "the seed plot of the Bible" for in it we have, in germ form, almost all of the great doctrines which are afterwards fully developed in the books of Scripture which follow... Religion/Inspirational Pages 420

☐ **The Master Key** *by L. W. de Laurence* ISBN: *1-59462-001-6* **$30.95**
In no branch of human knowledge has there been a more lively increase of the spirit of research during the past few years than in the study of Psychology, Concentration and Mental Discipline. The requests for authentic lessons in Thought Control, Mental Discipline and... New Age/Business Pages 422

☐ **The Lesser Key Of Solomon Goetia** *by L. W. de Laurence* ISBN: *1-59462-092-X* **$9.95**
This translation of the first book of the "Lernegton" which is now for the first time made accessible to students of Talismanic Magic was done, after careful collation and edition, from numerous Ancient Manuscripts in Hebrew, Latin, and French... New Age/Occult Pages 92

☐ **Rubaiyat Of Omar Khayyam** *by Edward Fitzgerald* ISBN: *1-59462-332-5* **$13.95**
Edward Fitzgerald, whom the world has already learned, in spite of his own efforts to remain within the shadow of anonymity, to look upon as one of the rarest poets of the century, was born at Bredfield, in Suffolk, on the 31st of March, 1809. He was the third son of John Purcell... Music Pages 172

☐ **Ancient Law** *by Henry Maine* ISBN: *1-59462-128-4* **$29.95**
The chief object of the following pages is to indicate some of the earliest ideas of mankind, as they are reflected in Ancient Law, and to point out the relation of those ideas to modern thought. Religion/History Pages 452

☐ **Far-Away Stories** *by William J. Locke* ISBN: *1-59462-129-2* **$19.45**
"Good wine needs no bush, but a collection of mixed vintages does. And this book is just such a collection. Some of the stories I do not want to remain buried for ever in the museum files of dead magazine-numbers an author's not unpardonable vanity..." Fiction Pages 272

☐ **Life of David Crockett** *by David Crockett* ISBN: *1-59462-250-7* **$27.45**
"Colonel David Crockett was one of the most remarkable men of the times in which he lived. Born in humble life, but gifted with a strong will, an indomitable courage, and unremitting perseverance... Biographies/New Age Pages 424

☐ **Lip-Reading** *by Edward Nitchie* ISBN: *1-59462-206-X* **$25.95**
Edward B. Nitchie, founder of the New York School for the Hard of Hearing, now the Nitchie School of Lip-Reading, Inc, wrote "LIP-READING Principles and Practice". The development and perfecting of this meritorious work on lip-reading was an undertaking... How-to Pages 400

☐ **A Handbook of Suggestive Therapeutics, Applied Hypnotism, Psychic Science** ISBN: *1-59462-214-0* **$24.95**
by Henry Munro Health/New Age/Health/Self-help Pages 376

☐ **A Doll's House: and Two Other Plays** *by Henrik Ibsen* ISBN: *1-59462-112-8* **$19.95**
Henrik Ibsen created this classic when in revolutionary 1848 Rome. Introducing some striking concepts in playwriting for the realist genre, this play has been studied the world over. Fiction/Classics/Plays 308

☐ **The Light of Asia** *by sir Edwin Arnold* ISBN: *1-59462-204-3* **$13.95**
In this poetic masterpiece, Edwin Arnold describes the life and teachings of Buddha. The man who was to become known as Buddha to the world was born as Prince Gautama of India but he rejected the worldly riches and abandoned the reigns of power when... Religion/History/Biographies Pages 170

☐ **The Complete Works of Guy de Maupassant** *by Guy de Maupassant* ISBN: *1-59462-157-8* **$16.95**
"For days and days, nights and nights, I had dreamed of that first kiss which was to consecrate our engagement, and I knew not on what spot I should put my lips..." Fiction/Classics Pages 240

☐ **The Art of Cross-Examination** *by Francis L. Wellman* ISBN: *1-59462-309-0* **$26.95**
Written by a renowned trial lawyer, Wellman imparts his experience and uses case studies to explain how to use psychology to extract desired information through questioning. How-to/Science/Reference Pages 408

☐ **Answered or Unanswered?** *by Louisa Vaughan* ISBN: *1-59462-248-5* **$10.95**
Miracles of Faith in China Religion Pages 112

☐ **The Edinburgh Lectures on Mental Science (1909)** *by Thomas* ISBN: *1-59462-008-3* **$11.95**
This book contains the substance of a course of lectures recently given by the writer in the Queen Street Hail, Edinburgh. Its purpose is to indicate the Natural Principles governing the relation between Mental Action and Material Conditions... New Age/Psychology Pages 148

☐ **Ayesha** *by H. Rider Haggard* ISBN: *1-59462-301-5* **$24.95**
Verily and indeed it is the unexpected that happens! Probably if there was one person upon the earth from whom the Editor of this, and of a certain previous history, did not expect to hear again... Classics Pages 380

☐ **Ayala's Angel** *by Anthony Trollope* ISBN: *1-59462-352-X* **$29.95**
The two girls were both pretty, but Lucy who was twenty-one who supposed to be simple and comparatively unattractive, whereas Ayala was credited, as her Bombwhat romantic name might show, with poetic charm and a taste for romance. Ayala when her father died was nineteen... Fiction Pages 484

☐ **The American Commonwealth** *by James Bryce* ISBN: *1-59462-286-8* **$34.45**
An interpretation of American democratic political theory. It examines political mechanics and society from the perspective of Scotsman James Bryce Politics Pages 572

☐ **Stories of the Pilgrims** *by Margaret P. Pumphrey* ISBN: *1-59462-116-0* **$17.95**
This book explores pilgrims religious oppression in England as well as their escape to Holland and eventual crossing to America on the Mayflower, and their early days in New England... History Pages 268

The Fasting Cure *by Sinclair Upton*   ISBN: *1-59462-222-1* **$13.95**
In the Cosmopolitan Magazine for May, 1910, and in the Contemporary Review (London) for April, 1910, I published an article dealing with my experiences in fasting. I have written a great many magazine articles, but never one which attracted so much attention... New Age/Self Help/Health Pages 164

Hebrew Astrology *by Sepharial*   ISBN: *1-59462-308-2* **$13.45**
In these days of advanced thinking it is a matter of common observation that we have left many of the old landmarks behind and that we are now pressing forward to greater heights and to a wider horizon than that which represented the mind-content of our progenitors... Astrology Pages 144

Thought Vibration or The Law of Attraction in the Thought World   ISBN: *1-59462-127-6* **$12.95**
by William Walker Atkinson   Psychology/Religion Pages 144

Optimism *by Helen Keller*   ISBN: *1-59462-108-X* **$15.95**
Helen Keller was blind, deaf, and mute since 19 months old, yet famously learned how to overcome these handicaps, communicate with the world, and spread her lectures promoting optimism. An inspiring read for everyone... Biographies/Inspirational Pages 84

Sara Crewe *by Frances Burnett*   ISBN: *1-59462-360-0* **$9.45**
In the first place, Miss Minchin lived in London. Her home was a large, dull, tall one, in a large, dull square, where all the houses were alike, and all the sparrows were alike, and where all the door-knockers made the same heavy sound... Childrens/Classic Pages 88

The Autobiography of Benjamin Franklin *by Benjamin Franklin*   ISBN: *1-59462-135-7* **$24.95**
The Autobiography of Benjamin Franklin has probably been more extensively read than any other American historical work, and no other book of its kind has had such ups and downs of fortune. Franklin lived for many years in England, where he was agent... Biographies/History Pages 332

Name	
Email	
Telephone	
Address	
City, State ZIP	

☐ **Credit Card**   ☐ **Check / Money Order**

Credit Card Number	
Expiration Date	
Signature	

Please Mail to: Book Jungle
PO Box 2226
Champaign, IL 61825
or Fax to: 630-214-0564

ORDERING INFORMATION

web*: www.bookjungle.com*
email*: sales@bookjungle.com*
fax*: 630-214-0564*
mail*: Book Jungle PO Box 2226 Champaign, IL 61825*
or PayPal *to sales@bookjungle.com*

Please contact us for bulk discounts

DIRECT-ORDER TERMS

**20% Discount if You Order
Two or More Books**
Free Domestic Shipping!
Accepted: Master Card, Visa,
Discover, American Express

www.ingramcontent.com/pod-product-compliance
Lightning Source LLC
Chambersburg PA
CBHW081232090426
42738CB00016B/3273